Beyond Your First Year in CTE:

10 ADDITIONAL THINGS to KNW

ISBN# 978-0-692-85569-0

Published by the Association for Career
and Technical Education

**Association for Career
and Technical Education
ACTE®**

1410 King Street Alexandria, VA 22314
Phone: 800-826-9972 // Fax: 703-683-7424
www.acteonline.org // *Connecting Education and Careers*

For information about this title or to order books and/or electronic media,
contact the publisher at info@acteonline.org.

Printed in the United States of America

Table of Contents

about the
Authors

In collaboration with ACTE, we would like to present our third book, focusing on things to know as a new career and technical educator, entitled *Beyond Your First Year in CTE: 10 Additional Things to Know*. You may have noticed from the cover of the book that we have added an additional author to our listing. The authors of this book, like the last two, represent well over 150 years of career and technical education (CTE) experience and come from a broad range of perspectives and specialties within this field. In addition, the contributing authors, again, represent 150 years, totaling over 300 years altogether.

Dr. Greg Belcher's studies in CTE enabled him to gain entry-level skills in both the welding and mechanical industries. He worked in both of these occupational areas before joining the ranks of the CTE teaching profession as a welding instructor at the community college level. As a faculty member, he developed an interest in CTE teacher preparation while assisting other adjunct faculty in their own professional development journey. This influenced him to pursue a Ph.D. in Comprehensive Vocational Education centered on CTE teacher preparation.

After completing his doctorate, he started teaching at Pittsburgh State University in the Technical Teacher Education program. The focus of this program was helping to prepare CTE instructors (at both the secondary and post-secondary levels) who were transitioning from business and industry to teaching in a CTE program/pathway.

Dr. Belcher has been an educator for the past 20 years. Two years ago, he became director of the newly-developed Kansas Career and Technical Education Center. This center's primary goal is to further development of secondary and post-secondary CTE teachers within the state of Kansas.

Dr. John Foster's career experience began when he was a tradesman in the construction industry. In the early years of the Vocational Education Acts, a community college career counselor asked John to visit a carpentry program in a regional school. Soon after that visit, he began his career in CTE as a carpentry teacher. At the time, John was a bit of a rarity as a starting teacher: he had a bachelor's degree in vocational education. He later earned a master's degree in vocational education administration and became a CTE director at the secondary level.

Dr. Foster completed a Ph.D. in workforce development and began work in CTE teacher education. It was in these two positions that he witnessed the positive power of instructional improvement through the objective use of data. Dr. Foster took a position as a state director of CTE and served three different governors. Dr. Foster also formed relationships with a number of key researchers in the field of CTE; among them were Dr. Ken Gray, Dr. Neil (Mac) McCaslin, and Dr. James Stone. Dr. Foster credits the many stars of CTE that he has met along the way for sharing their expertise, and hopes his experiences will benefit those reading this book.

In 2005, Dr. Foster took the helm of NOCTI, formerly the National Occupational Competency Testing Institute. While there, he has forged strong ties with Advance CTE, formerly the National Association of State Directors of Career and Technical Education consortium (NASDCTEc), and the Association of Career and Technical Education (ACTE).

Dr. Pamela Foster obtained her bachelor's and master's degrees in science education, and later a Ph.D. in workforce education and development. She taught in a comprehensive (academic and CTE) high school for 34 years, during which she was also the science program chair for 12 years. As a science representative, Dr. Foster worked with and mentored academic and CTE educators to create motivating, integrated lessons and units. She has shared her experiences and practices at local, state and national conferences.

Dr. Foster has facilitated webinars for the Southern Regional Education Board (SREB) and has also been responsible for planning integrated nationwide professional development activities. She was recognized in 1991 as a semi-finalist for state teacher of the year, and in 2010 was recognized by the state of Pennsylvania as the outstanding biology teacher. Although retired, Dr. Foster continues to mentor new CTE teachers and volunteers with the Audubon Society in teaching grade school students about STEM-related issues, including stream ecology and conservation.

Dr. Clyde Hornberger is a dynamic leader whose wide-ranging list of experiences include the institution of competency-based instruction in the largest technical program in the state of Pennsylvania. He served as Executive Director of Lehigh Career and Technical Institute for over 15 years, where he doubled their offerings and established the school as a national model. Dr. Hornberger also served as President of the Pennsylvania Association of Career and Technical Administrators (PACTA) and on the executive boards of the school board association, the Manufacturing Skill

Standards Council (MSSC), and the SkillsUSA leadership council. He earned his doctorate in education at Temple University and previously held teaching and administrative assignments in CTE in Schuylkill and Berks Counties. During these same years, Dr. Hornberger also served in the U.S. Army Reserves attaining the rank of Colonel.

Now retired from that post, Colonel Hornberger still maintains the discipline and outcome focus that he learned throughout his military career. Dr. Hornberger served as special advisor to the Pennsylvania Secretary of Education for almost 10 years. He was appointed to the Pennsylvania House of Representatives Keystone Commission on Education for Employment for the 21st Century. He also has served as chair of the NOCTI board of directors.

Dr. Hornberger's focus through all of his experiences has been to enhance the educational and career opportunities for youth, incumbent workers, and adults. He currently serves as an educational consultant specializing in CTE and has consulted for the school districts of Philadelphia, Little Rock, St. Louis, Anchorage, Omaha, and a variety of others.

setting the
Stage

Because of the shortage of qualified CTE teachers, we began a project with our friends at ACTE three years ago. The shortage of teachers from both traditional sources (colleges and universities), and alternative sources, (the workplace) has led to states using a variety of incentives and "fast-track" programs to obtain individuals with technical competence so they can transfer their knowledge and skills to CTE students. Unfortunately, in some states around the country, the ongoing education of these CTE teachers has been limited or, in some cases, ignored. At a time in our history when new technologies, new materials, and new processes seem to be emerging every day, the focus on teaching technical skills to work in these fields couldn't be greater and demands a commitment to continuous learning.

When it comes to preparing our future workforce, however, technical skills are only half of the story. Without an understanding of how people learn, or a good grasp of the best strategies for the motivation and mechanisms for monitoring and rewarding individual success, we handicap those delivering technical skills to our students. We believe that ongoing professional development, encompassing both educational and technical strategies, combined with a system of ongoing mentoring, is CTE teachers' best hope for success. We believe that the experiences of the authors of each of the three books written, amassing over 150 years in CTE teaching, teacher training, administration, and policy-making, should be helpful. These books are not meant to be a "cure all." They are intended to be easy to read, lighthearted resources for anyone involved in CTE program delivery.

Your First Year in CTE: 10 Things to Know focused on the first three months of an individual's new teaching career. That is a time when new CTE teachers are frequently bombarded with problems and situations that they did not anticipate. Even with the benefit of a four-year degree in teaching pedagogy, new teachers generally find themselves consumed by day-to-day activities and find it difficult to make time to implement a long-range plan. These new teachers are still uncertain as to what strategies will work with their students. It is important to note that alternatively-certified CTE teachers have not had the benefit of a degree in education methodology, and also may not have had any kind of student-teaching experience.

Our first and second books also discussed how CTE teachers are a special breed. The factors that account for that "specialness" may also account for some of the frustration experienced in that first year. The second book, *Your First Year in CTE, 10 MORE Things to Know*, is still about a teacher's first year in CTE teaching. We have chosen in this third book to reiterate how this "specialness" can be a mixed blessing, and have repeated a small section about the characteristics of CTE teachers from our first and second books.

- CTE teachers typically start their teaching career at an older age than most general education teachers. This may mean that they have gotten accustomed to what have been, up until this point, routines that have made them effective and efficient at their individual occupations. Suddenly they may no longer be effective—see why they might be frustrated?
- CTE teachers typically bring many years of content experience with them before they enter the classroom. That content experience, however, is not in education, and suddenly they can't rely on the background that made them successful in their former careers.
- CTE teachers make a substantial career change to enter the classroom. Many times, they are at the top of their particular fields, and then transition into a career they know little about.
- CTE teachers make a commitment to a lifetime of education. Not only do they have to stay current with the technical field they left, but they must also play "catch up" in their new field. In many states, alternatively-credentialed CTE teachers have to acquire a substantial number of college credits in teaching pedagogy while simultaneously working in a new education field.

These four differences alone create a ripple of effects that makes it more difficult for CTE teachers to navigate their new environment.

The first book was targeted at new CTE teachers who need help developing relationships and surviving the first three months. We mentioned that, without proper support, early difficulties may cause those entering their new field to give up and return to their former careers. Even those that have support and a good initial "launch" may end up working so hard that "burn-out" becomes a real issue. The research literature and folklore surrounding CTE teaching indicates that this attrition occurs in the first three to four years for new teachers.

Our second book, *Your First Year in CTE, 10 MORE Things to Know*, maintained that "easy and fun" read approach for newer CTE teachers. It focused on details that teachers need to use year in and year out such as lesson planning, test development, end-of-year inventories and reflections, and making connections with parents, among other topics. It maintained "hands-on" examples and references, both packed with ideas that could be adapted for CTE classrooms.

This third book shifts the focus a bit. It assumes that the new CTE teacher has come far enough to decide that teaching is definitely for him or her. The teacher has built relationships and his or her students have started to experience success after leaving the CTE classroom. Now is the time to think about responsibilities to the CTE profession.

Beyond Your First Year in CTE: 10 Additional Things to Know discusses issues like the impact of federal and state legislation on the CTE classroom, visibility in the community, and becoming a leader. We've maintained the informative yet lighthearted style and, again, filled the chapters with information, regardless of the CTE field taught.

We know CTE teachers are a special breed, and we want to be able to pass along information to help you become a successful and professional CTE educator, just like our mentors have done for us! We share your passion, and welcome you to the ranks of CTE professionals across the country.

chapter I

Your Classroom and Federal Legislation

Life Under the Big Top!

This first chapter discusses something that is usually pretty far-removed from most teachers' classrooms: federal legislation. In a way, CTE teachers have a sort of dedicated federal funding stream. The underlying reason for this legislation is the need for a prepared workforce and the impact that said workforce has on the economy and on our standard of living. CTE professionals need to have some context surrounding that legislation. They need to know how it evolved, how it can help them, and what they have to do to maintain it.

You were hired for your content expertise and your knowledge, skill, and experience in your particular technical field. You've had to develop your educational knowledge over your initial years in the CTE classroom. In our first book, *Your First Year in CTE, 10 Things to Know*, we discussed establishing initial relationships; in our second book, *Your First Year in CTE, 10 MORE Things to Know*, we discussed everyday educational tools; and in this book we are focusing on the process of becoming a professional. A lot of becoming a professional has to do with knowing your field, your classroom, your school, and the influences acting upon them. So our intention here is to discuss the impacts of federal legislation on your classroom, not the legislation itself.

We really don't have the space or time to discuss all of the history surrounding CTE over the years, and there are plenty of better historical references for that. It is important to understand that the development of technically-skilled workers has been the subject of federal legislation for many years. As such, we've compiled a very brief list of some of the major laws over the last century:

- **1917: Smith-Hughes Act:** Provided federal resources for establishing vocational programs in agriculture, home economics, and trade and industrial education at the secondary level.
- **1936: George-Deen Act:** Provided federal resources establishing additional vocational areas, including distributive (marketing) occupations and teacher-education programs.
- **1958: National Defense Education Act:** Provided additional federal support for states and local schools, enabling them to strengthen science and mathematics, and also provided funds to support technical programs and vocational guidance.
- **1963: Vocational Education Act of 1963:** Provided federal funds to support the construction of vocational schools, vocational work-study programs, research, training, and demonstrations in vocational education programming.
- **1968: Vocational Education Amendments of 1968:** Placed an additional federal emphasis on vocational programs at the post-secondary level and added the field of cooperative education.
- **1976: Vocational Education Amendments of 1976:** Focused on serving special populations and the basic skills program (improving achievement in reading, mathematics, and written and oral communication.)
- **1984: Carl D. Perkins Vocational Education Act:** Supported improving, modernizing, and developing quality vocational education programs. Included goals for economic growth and continued focus on serving specific populations, including students with disabilities and disadvantaged individuals.

- **1990: Carl D. Perkins Vocational and Applied Technology Education Act:** Focused on vocational opportunities for disadvantaged individuals and teaching all students the skills and competencies necessary to work in a technologically-advanced society. It provided initial funding for the integration of academic and vocational education and for Tech Prep programs.
- **1998: Carl D. Perkins Vocational and Technical Education Act:** Provided greater flexibility to develop CTE programs while increasing student performance accountability.
- **2006: Carl D. Perkins Career and Technical Education Act:** Provided support for improving academic achievement of CTE students, strengthening the connections between secondary and post-secondary education, and improving state and local accountability.

 Generally speaking, each iteration of CTE federal funding broadened the scope of technical areas covered by the legislation, and the populations included within. In the last few iterations, you'll also notice an increasing focus on accountability and academic achievement. One can draw many parallels to what was happening in American history and in society when each piece of legislation was drafted, but what's important to you as a new CTE professional educator is not only being aware of the context, but also knowing the impact of the current legislation on your classroom.

Carl D. Perkins CTE Act of 2006

One of the primary influences regarding CTE legislation has on your classroom is the funding it provides! CTE funding at the local school level comes from three main sources: federal, state, and local funding.

 Though federal funding is by far the smallest revenue source for most schools, usually hovering between 5 and 15 percent, it is important because it provides flexible funding that allows for program improvements and innovations. Since federal law often impacts state policy priorities as well, some see federal dollars as the primary agents of change and standardization across the United States.

So how does this chain of funding work? Through a formula outlined in the law, all states get a portion of the congressional appropriations provided under the legislation. The two main contributing variables are state population and average income. Generally, the larger the population of the state, and the lower its income, the higher the dollar amount. California, for example, gets the largest appropriation of any of the states, due to the size of its population. Once states receive their grants each year, 85 percent of that funding is passed directly to local school districts and post-secondary institutions through another population-and-poverty-based formula.

In order to receive its share of the funding, a local school district or post-secondary institution has to meet a series of requirements. These requirements are spelled out in the section of the law on the local plan and are sometimes called a "local application." States can also add additional prerequisites to those required by federal law, so how this process unfolds from state to state varies. Generally, though, local recipients have to ensure that they are offering CTE programs and activities of sufficient size, scope, and quality to be effective. Some states also require specific program approval for things like maintaining local industry relationships, overseeing the upkeep of safe facilities, and hiring certified teachers. Your local CTE administrator or a mentor teacher can help you locate what your state requires.

At the secondary level, once a school district receives its Perkins allocation, it can use any number of methods for distributing funding to individual schools or CTE programs. It may divide funding equally among schools/programs in the district, set priority areas across the district to be funded each year, or even run a separate local competition in which programs apply for a share of the funding. This varies even within states, so it is very important to find out how it works in your school district so you will know how you can get access to the funding.

You should be aware of the other critical piece of the law: accountability requirements, or what it takes to maintain the flow of federal dollars. The federal Office of Career, Technical and Adult Education (OCTAE) maintains a staff of individuals whose job it is to assure that federal dollars are being spent properly by individual states. These individuals visit state offices during the duration of the legislation and see that each state is following its plan for allocating expenditures.

OCTAE also helps set state accountability requirements and verifies reports that are submitted annually on something called the Consolidated Annual Report (CAR; Perkins Collaborative Resource Network, 2016a). The CAR contains financial data, along with information on student enrollment and performance on key measures outlined in the law. That performance is reported in the following categories:

Secondary Level:

1S1: Academic Attainment in Reading/Language Arts
1S2: Academic Attainment in Mathematics
2S1: Technical Skill Attainment
3S1: Secondary School Completion
4S1: Student Graduation Rate
5S1: Secondary Placement
6S1: Nontraditional Participation
6S2: Nontraditional Completion

Post-secondary Level:

1P1: Technical Skill Attainment
2P1: Credential, Certificate or Diploma
3P1: Student Retention or Transfer
4P1: Student Placement
5P1: Nontraditional Participation
5P2: Nontraditional Completion

Your state sets performance goals in each of these areas, generally expressed as the percentage of CTE students that meet a particular target (like high school graduation), and is required to report on the results to the federal government. In turn, each local school district and post-secondary institution has to set its own target performance goals, with the approval of the state, and report on its performance each year. Individual classroom numbers are very important to your district/institution performance, and get aggregated in the state as well.

As a CTE teacher, you should be working to influence the indicators related to your level of education. For example, you have a direct impact on 2S1: technical skill attainment at the secondary level, and 1P1: technical skill attainment at the post-secondary level. While each state defines exactly how this technical skill attainment is measured, generally "success" on this measure includes students passing end-of-program technical assessments or earning industry-recognized credentials. Ultimately, how your students score on these assessments helps to maintain the federal flow of dollars to your school and to your classroom.

You'll want to assure both that your students can meet nationally accepted industry standards and that they are prepared to achieve success on whatever industry credential is used as a metric for your technical program. As a CTE professional, you must also do your part to contribute to performance on other measures of the CAR. For example, academic-CTE integration (discussed in Chapter V) can reinforce academic skills necessary for performance on other assessments used for high school graduation.

Similarly, your state likely has individuals that visit local schools using federal CTE dollars to assure not only federal compliance, but state compliance requirements as well, and you may have additional state performance-reporting requirements. These individuals will typically want to spend time with CTE school administrators, as well as some time in CTE classrooms. Your facility and program should always be ready to receive visitors—and these visitors, who may be in control of any state dollars that your school or program may receive, are extremely important.

Impacts of Other Federal Monies: WIOA

In 2014, the Workforce Investment Act was reauthorized as the Workforce Innovation and Opportunity Act (WIOA). It is one of the main federal laws that have an impact on CTE and can help to provide resources. Perkins has already been discussed; in addition to WIOA, another key piece of legislation is the Elementary and Secondary Education Act, also known as the "Every Student Succeeds Act" (ESSA). The Individuals with Disabilities Education Act also impacts how CTE programs serve students with disabilities (covered in our last book, *Your First Year in CTE, 10 More Things to Know*).

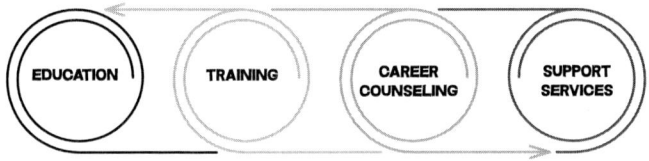

Through a system of state and local workforce development boards and One-Stop career centers (Perkins Collaborative Resource Network, 2016b), WIOA supports job training, workforce development activities, and adult education programs As with Perkins, there are requirements for stakeholder involvement—one of those stakeholders (maybe you) could be from the CTE community. The WIOA legislation requires states to develop career pathways. These pathways are a combination of education, training, career counseling, and support services that align with the skill needs of industries. WIOA also provides for more standard performance measures across job training programs, which have the potential to shift how data is collected and aligned in CTE.

WIOA-funded One-Stop centers can serve as a resource for your individual CTE classroom. These centers have current labor market data, access to local employer workforce needs, and training resources. WIOA youth programs are required to provide work experiences for young adults, and this can benefit your work-based learning programs. WIOA programs also have funds available to help offset post-secondary training costs for some populations of individuals. Perhaps you can find local occupational advisory members in WIOA's database of employers, or cooperative education placements, or short-term paid internships, for your students.

Impacts of Other Federal Monies: ESSA

The last piece of federal legislation to be discussed is the Every Student Succeeds Act (ESSA, 2015). This law, the latest reauthorization of the

Elementary and Secondary Education Act, was signed in 2015 and requires all students to be taught to high academic standards that will help them succeed in college and careers (Perkins Collaborative Resource Network, 2016c). It provides unprecedented support for CTE by including CTE in a definition of a "well-rounded education," and offers numerous opportunities for including CTE in state and local plans. In addition, states can include career readiness measures in state accountability systems, and state report cards can contain information on the progress of students obtaining CTE competencies. ACTE's handouts have been adapted by the authors and provide a list of potential opportunities for your classroom. Listed below are some potential initiatives funds could be used for:

- Helping develop coordinated instructional strategies between CTE teachers and regular education counterparts, such as through common planning time
- Offering experiential and work-based learning
- Supporting student transition from middle school to high school and from high school to post-secondary education
- Integrating CTE into comprehensive literacy instruction
- Expanding access to technology used in the CTE classroom
- Helping to promote career awareness and expand career exploration activities
- Increasing training for counselors on labor market information and employer needs
- Helping students obtain career readiness skills
- Accessing specialized professional development for both regular education and CTE teachers; and
- Assisting with articulation agreements to post-secondary education and dual and concurrent enrollment programs.

Tools For Your Toolbox

The first "tool" in this section comes from a law enforcement teacher in Maine and discusses special needs legislation (covered in an earlier book in this series, *Your First Year in CTE, 10 More Things to Know)*. This teacher's reflection underscores how important it is for CTE teachers to be aware of federal legislation requirements, regardless of the focus of the legislation.

Like a lot of new teachers, I entered the world of CTE in 2008 with extensive trade experience and abundant enthusiasm, but without a teaching degree. In my career as a police officer, I taught seasoned professionals in an academy setting, and I had to focus on documenting attendance, following a rigid lesson plan, and meeting learning objectives for adult learners. As I quickly learned, teaching adolescents in a career and technical program is a "whole other animal."

In Maine, state law allows alternative pathways to teacher certification. After retirement, I was granted conditional certification based on my college degrees and my work experience. One of the most important college courses that I have ever taken was on "Exceptionality for the Diverse Learner." Thankfully, I completed this course before setting foot in my classroom for the first time. I learned a lot about federal legislation like IDEA, FAPE, and NCLB [what is now ESSA]. As the parent of a child with a learning disability, I was familiar with an IEP and the annual review process, but this course laid out federal requirements for compliance in a clear, succinct manner. Having this information in hand helped me immensely when I "jumped into the frying pan" on my first day of teaching.

As a rookie teacher, with no formal student teaching experience, I was excited and terrified every day, but I was confident because I knew about relevant federal legislation and focused my efforts on complying with the letter of the law, while never losing sight of its spirit. Federal legislation on public school education was passed to afford every American child, regardless of his or her cognitive ability or learning disability, the best chance to learn today in order to succeed tomorrow. The legal requirements for education serve as both a barometer and a blueprint for ordering your teaching to best meet the needs of every child. Don't fear federal legislation; embrace it and use it to challenge yourself to be a better teacher. Somewhere out there is a child that needs you to care about them, educate them, and be a positive influence in their life. You may be all that they have. Do right by them.

This second reflection is from a CTE administrator in a large CTE center in Massachusetts, and discusses how federal legislation can help you achieve your classroom goals.

Perkins legislation is the single biggest federal law that contains appropriations from Washington to local schools for CTE. How much your school receives depends upon the state you live in and the demographics of your school district/community. In smaller districts, for example, the amount of money could be quite small, perhaps $15,000. But in larger districts, it could be very large—hundreds of thousands of dollars, or even millions. The important thing to remember is this: Your school receives federal monies that can be used to help you in your classroom, lab, or shop.

Have you ever been told, "There's no money in our budget for that!" when you inquired about a new cutting-edge piece of equipment or about attending a national conference to learn about innovations in your trade? If so, <u>think Perkins</u>. Ask your supervisor, director or principal about the availability of Perkins funds. Those federal dollars are intended to be used to **supplement** the local budget, not **supplant** it (that is, replace it). Put another way, Perkins' dollars need to be spent for something not already in the local budget, something "extra" designed to modernize or improve your program.

Another tip: Once you find out who actually oversees the Perkins plan for your school district, talk to that person. Let them know that you are always available to discuss ideas on how to allocate available funds. Discuss Perkins with your occupational advisory committee and make sure they understand its potential to improve the program. Offer your local Perkins' administrator assistance from the advisory committee if equipment quotes, letters of support, or simple phone calls are needed to discuss the development of the local Perkins plan. In most cases, the admin-

istrator will be happy to hear from you. Throughout the year, that person will be far more likely to think of <u>you</u> when making any last-minute decisions on where to spend. Speak up!

One more thing—you may hear other staff grumbling about federal programs that require excessive reporting that seems irrelevant to your day-to-day experience or which appears to be tangling with local politics. It is true that reporting can be a burden, but that's what administrators are equipped to handle. On the front lines of learning, effective administrative policies can help you achieve the goals you have set with your students. It's worth the time to read some of the summaries of federal policy that are available through professional teachers' organizations, like ACTE or its regional or state affiliate.

The final entry in the toolbox comes to us from a policy advisor within the Wisconsin technical college system. Speaking from a bigger picture perspective, she discusses the importance of federal legislation, underscoring the importance of understanding how it connects to your classroom. The reflection also provides good advice about becoming an advocate.

Many state laws are enacted in response to federal legislation. The more familiar you are with federal laws, the more you'll understand the basis for your own state's laws and where they may differ. Federal laws also guide the use of federal funding. If you are receiving funding from a federal program, you should be familiar with the statutory purposes behind the program. Federal legislation sets direction. Although policy innovations may begin in a single state, they spread when that policy is codified into law on a national level. If you want to see which way the wind is blowing, follow the debate and the positions taken by various groups surrounding the enactment of that federal legislation.

Having spent a number of years working on various policy issues at the state and federal level, I am always somewhat surprised at how few educators are familiar with the federal legislation that impacts their classroom. Perhaps it's because for most of us,—save for a few CSPAN junkies—the events on Capitol Hill seem removed from what happens in our local statehouses. I guess I shouldn't be so surprised that most state-level news media don't even have a Washington, DC correspondent dedicated to covering Congress.

The good news is that it's easier than ever to follow developments in federal CTE policy and legislation by subscribing to online newsletters and social media posts from professional organizations, key congressional committees, and even your own representative in Congress.

Professional Development, Networking, and Advocacy

If you find that you enjoy following federal legislation, you might consider becoming involved in a professional organization with a committee devoted to federal CTE policy. It's a great opportunity to network with like-minded individuals in your state as well as throughout the country. You might even consider becoming an advocate. Being an advocate on a national level and having the opportunity to effect change is exciting. It also carries with it great responsibility. It isn't for beginners; you'll need to understand both the issues and the political landscape (and any boundaries) in which you operate.

Those of you who go on and become active in national professional organizations may, by virtue of your knowledge and expertise on CTE issues, find yourself asked to write a letter to your congressperson, to contribute to a national newsletter, or even to testify on issues before

Congress. Just be sure that you check in with the appropriate person(s) to find out how such requests are handled. You'll want to know if your district employs a federal lobbyist, or has government relations staff, and consult with them as necessary.

Your professional organization may have a position on a federal issue that is contrary to the stance taken by your local superintendent, state director of education, and/or governor. In such instances, you'll want to carefully consider the ramifications of taking a contrary position, if any, and always be clear whom you represent.

KEY LEARNINGS:

1. Know your place in "the big picture."
2. CTE has been federally supported since 1917; history and context are important.
3. Federal legislation combined with federal dollars influence the structure and operation of our programs..
4. You can help maintain the flow of federal dollars to your classroom.
5. Expect federal and state compliance visitors in your classroom.
6. There are several pieces of federal education legislation that are important to CTE teachers; the main legislation for CTE is the Perkins Act.
7. WIOA focuses on career pathways and job training.
8. ESSA contains many opportunities for CTE teachers to collaborate with other educators.

RELATED CONTENT THAT MAY BE OF INTEREST:

Carl D. Perkins Career and Technical Education Act of 2006 (Perkins IV). Public Law 109-270.

Elementary and Secondary Education Act (Every Student Succeeds Act). (2015). S. 1177—114th Congress: PL 114-95. Retrieved from https://www.gpo.gov/fdsys/pkg/BILLS-114s1177enr/pdf/BILLS-114s1177enr.pdf.

Perkins Collaborative Resource Network. (2016a). Accountability: Annual reporting. Washington, DC: U.S. Department of Education. Available at http://cte.ed.gov/accountability/annual-reporting.

Perkins Collaborative Resource Network. (2016b). Legislation: Workforce Innovation and Opportunity Act (WIOA). Washington, DC: U.S. Department of Education. Available at http://cte.ed.gov/legislation/about-wioa.

Perkins Collaborative Resource Network. (2016c). Legislation: Every Student Succeeds Act (ESSA). Washington, DC: U.S. Department of Education. Available at http://cte.ed.gov/legislation/about-essa.

Workforce Innovation and Opportunity Act (WIOA). (2014). Public Law 113-128 (29 U.S.C. Sec. 3101, et. seq.). Retrieved from https://www.congress.gov/113/plaws/publ128/PLAW-113publ128.pdf.

chapter II

The Greater CTE Community

It Takes a Village

"Leave this world a little better than you found it."
Robert Baden-Powell, circa 1941

"Planning is bringing the future into the present so that you can do something about it now."
Alan Lakein (1989)

Robert Baden-Powell isn't the only one to discuss the importance of making a positive contribution to the world around you, just as Alan Lakein wasn't the first to discuss the importance of looking ahead. Most would agree that it's part of human nature to want to improve one's surroundings, to want to be with those who have similar philosophies and ideas to our own, and to think about where we might find ourselves five years down the road. That feeling of being a part of something bigger than yourself, the knowledge that others must also have experienced

24

these frustrations, and the belief that there is power in numbers are all pretty common to the human psyche.

In the last chapter, we mentioned our partner ACTE, the part they play on the national stage, and their important role as advocates for the CTE community. In this chapter, we'll focus on identifying similar groups, both formal and informal, and on the benefits of participation. We will point out that, belonging to these kinds of groups is about more than the benefits that you accrue. It's about your obligation of participation; it's about contributing to your profession.

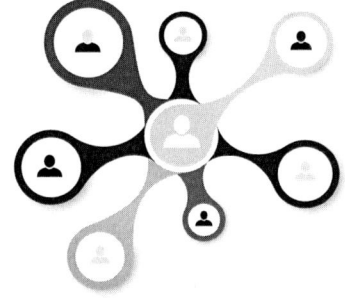

One could liken this concept to that of being a good citizen of a democracy. As a citizen of the United States you not only have the liberty, protection, and services the government provides, but you also feel a part of something bigger—something that you want to be a part of, and in some fashion, be a contributor to. That contribution reflects more than a financial contribution. It reflects contributions of time, talent, and participation.

Becoming a Professional

Perhaps your first teaching job involved some sort of relocation to an area where you didn't have a local network of experts from which to draw. One of the first things that a new CTE teacher may have to do is establish a viable occupational advisory committee (OAC). (We discussed this in *Your First Year in CTE: 10 MORE Things to Know*, by Foster, Foster, Hornberger & McNally, 2015.) A teacher has to find a way to know whether his or her instruction is valued by the community in which it is being delivered.

In all probability, you are likely already a member of a national association or state organization that represents your occupation and/or industry. You can contact the association for information about local chapters, or you can reach out individually. You can check with others, or just maybe you'll get lucky and find some sort of a localized trade association. By joining that local trade association, you will be able to develop a new network of professionals who can help you perfect your instruction.

After you have gotten to know the members of their local trade association, along with their goals and values, maybe you'll decide to participate in the leadership of this organization (see Chapter IX of Foster et al., 2015). Perhaps this organization has a regional or state affiliate; this expands your network even farther. An organization like this may also have national or international organizations. There may also be scholarships, internships, co-operative education slots, curriculum resources, and opportunities for students to participate in skill demonstrations. Maybe the organization assembles statewide shows or fairs. The point is this: unless you reach out and become involved in these kinds of organizations, you are missing important resources for both your development and that of your program's students. Professionals are active and engaged!

These are some benefits of participating in these sorts of groups:

- **Building your professional network:** As described in the first book CTE teaching can be a lonely profession. Most CTE teachers, unlike math or English teachers, are the only subject matter experts in their building, and maybe even in their county! That means that the chances to bounce subject-specific instructional strategies off someone else are pretty limited. Belonging to professional organizations to network and develop relationships can help fill this void. Also, sharing or asking for help with teaching strategies, ideas, lab activities, projects, etc., can be extremely helpful to the new CTE teacher. Even experienced educators can benefit since they should always be striving to improve their curriculum to best prepare their students.

- **Becoming a professional:** Some would define professionalism with words like respect, consideration, and honesty (Post, 2014). To the authors, it also means being a contributing citizen of whatever group you choose.

- **Improving personal and leadership skills:** Additional opportunities for professional development often become more available through networking with other people and organizations (Zetlin, 2014).

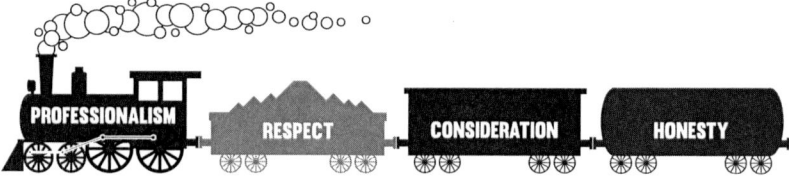

- **Promoting a sense of belonging to a larger group of professionals similar to you:** Belonging to a larger group can, and often does, improve group effectiveness toward achieving common goals.

- **Utilizing the power of groups:** Groups of like-minded individuals sometimes have similar needs. National groups may give you access to better purchasing power for a piece of equipment (discounts), or maybe more personal things, like term life insurance or discounts for hotel stays during professional development conferences. Some professional organizations, such as ACTE, offer complimentary common carrier accidental death and dismemberment insurance, plus discounted rates on professional liability and other insurance offerings.

- **Finding resources for your instruction:** Building-level administrators can help find many educational resources for the general teaching population, but where do you, a CTE instructor, go if you want to assess virtual welding equipment? What if you want to find the most efficient way to adhere an acrylic fingernail? Some of the organizations listed later in this chapter may prove more helpful than a Google search.

- **Finding opportunities for your students:** By networking with large organizations, you may have access to scholarships and/or internships for your students. Maybe the group can provide information that forecasts a new specialty within your field in which your students would be interested.

- **Accessing professional development options:** Do you have a mechanism for staying current in your field? Do you have access to postings by professional groups associated with your field, combined with the field of education? As a professional in CTE, you should!

- **Seeing future directions:** You are preparing the workforce of the future. How do you do that when you are working with training from the past? Technology of all kinds has accelerated the need for constant upskilling. A group may give you a sense of where your field is going and how you can help better prepare your students.

- **Giving back to your community:** Groups and organizations, regardless of their size and level, have expectations of people who join them. Whether the group is technically or educationally focused, that group expects and deserves your input. You are receiving benefits from belonging. It's only fair for the group to expect some individual contribution in return.

- **Increasing professional recognition:** Opportunities become more available for developing leadership, responsibility, self-confidence and recognition in the school, state, and/or national communities when you're a member of a professional organization.
- **Promoting career awareness:** Career awareness and possible opportunities for advancement become available with professional networking.
- **Receiving professional or trade journals:** It can be inspiring and helpful to a young teacher to receive professional CTE journals packed full of helpful tips, relevant articles, etc., that delve into CTE trends, case studies, and in-classroom innovations, too.

Professional Organizations

The following section lists the types of groups that you might want to participate in, and provides a few examples of each:

- **Multi-level national industry associations:** Such organizations not only have a national presence, but also one that maintains affiliates at other levels—regional, statewide, local, and perhaps even international. Depending on the organization's focus, CTE teachers generally start their involvement with a local chapter. There may be more activity at this level, and by becoming involved, you may join others that work in your school or community. Don't forget to consider the benefits of these organizations' broader focus. Consider expanded opportunities to demonstrate leadership and to find professional development opportunities. Consider, too, the expanded networking opportunities as well as opportunities to provide other employment. These kinds of opportunities can be provided by a specific job board or simply by word of mouth among the network of members.
- **ACTE:** This is one of those multi-level national organizations explained above, but with a different focus, namely serving the needs of all CTE professionals. This service includes membership services, lobbying, professional development, and a host of opportunities for networking and leadership. Frankly, membership in ACTE should be a requirement of all CTE professionals. You can find more about the benefits of membership by going to www.acteonline.org. ACTE also has a benefit called "educational institution membership," or EIM in which your entire school becomes a member of ACTE. You may want to review the benefits

of this type of affiliation. Benefits include free event registrations and publications. Encourage your supervisors to join.

- **Groups that stretch your thinking:** Being outside of your comfort zone is almost always a good strategy for professional growth. Think about groups whose mission involves something in which you have an interest. You might consider joining a group that is focused on learning a new language, a new skill, or which works to implement new instructional technologies. Or maybe a group with an eye on the future like the World Future Society might interest you.

- **College coursework:** Most alternatively-certified CTE teachers start their new careers without a degree in teaching. As they move through their careers, it is important to stay current with new strategies for teaching to gain the context for teaching that some of their peers who have come through more traditional routes already have. Frequently, both formal and informal groups are associated with college coursework. Along with alumni organizations, you may want to consider education-specific groups within these institutions.

- **ACTER:** A group called the Association for Career and Technical Education Research (ACTER) consists of individuals who research career-technical educational issues. Their publications can provide a source of the latest studies and discussion of issues in CTE. See acteronline.org for membership information.

- **Advance CTE:** If your interest is in policy development and the implementation of federal legislation, you might want to consider taking a serious look at Advance CTE. Every state and U.S. territory has someone serving in a director's role. Typically, these are individuals housed at a state office who are charged with CTE policy and rulemaking. They usually provide oversight regarding the implementation of the Carl D. Perkins federal legislation. Advance CTE is an organization dedicated to individuals in those positions. However, they also have a category of membership called an associate membership for individuals (e.g., teachers and administrators) who are part of the educational delivery system.

- **NOCTI:** Most CTE practitioners don't consider NOCTI a membership organization that one "joins." They consider NOCTI a provider of industry-driven credentials. However, NOCTI is a membership organization for states and it has no membership fee! All state directors in Advance CTE are also members of NOCTI. The active membership in NOCTI is maintained not through a dues structure but by a contribution of services to

NOCTI. One of those contributions is to provide NOCTI with two subject matter experts per year. You can assist in the development and updating of industry credentials by nominating your occupational advisory members at nocti.org/SME.cfm, by agreeing to be a subject matter expert or independent reviewer, by providing a pilot site for credential validation (nocti.org/PilotTesting.cfm) or by affirming that you, as a CTE professional, understand all aspects of your particular industry by taking a teacher test (see the teacher testing information at nocti.org/ATC.cfm). You can also benefit from information provided on the Teachers' Corner at http://nocti.org/TeachersCorner.cfm.

- **Administrator organizations:** Depending on your location and state, a number of groups exist for individuals who either have the desire to move into CTE administration or who just want to have a better understanding of the way an education system is governed. There are local CTE directors' associations like this one in Pennsylvania (PACTA at www.pacareertech.org) or this one in Missouri with materials for administrators (http://www.missouricareereducation.org/home.php). There are also secondary principals' groups, middle school principals' groups, and even counselors' groups that might be of interest to you.

- **Technical content-area teacher groups:** Some states have CTE content-area groups. These groups may meet only once or twice a year, or they may even just meet virtually, but the benefits of sharing tips and techniques specific to your content are well worth the effort to attend. Examples are groups like statewide cosmetology teachers' groups or welding teachers' groups. If you are unaware of a group's existence in your state, maybe it's time to reach out and form one yourself!

- **WIOA (Workforce Investment Opportunities Act)-related groups:** All states have a mechanism for delivering WIOA services; here's one example from the state of Illinois (https://www.illinoisworknet.com/). A formal or an informal look at their services and how they relate to what you do in your community may be an "eye-opener" and an educational opportunity for both you and your students.

- **Career and Technical Student Organizations (CTSOs):** These were mentioned in both Cole, Foster, Foster & McNally (2014, p. 12 & chapter IX) and Foster et al. (2015, Chapter IV), so a lot of detail is not needed here. Remember that CTSOs are not only great organizations for your students, but they also can provide significant networking, leadership, and professional development opportunities for CTE professionals who choose to get involved.

Tools For Your Toolbox

Our first reflection comes from a state administrator in California who discusses the benefits of belonging to ACTE:

I currently serve as a state administrator for CTE. As I reflect back to when I was a new classroom teacher, if I had been asked about ACTE, I would not have had a clue what the organization was about. It wasn't until about the fifth year in my teaching CTE that a colleague introduced me to ACTE, and I decided to join the organization. It turned out to be one of the best professional decisions I could have made as a CTE educator. I believe that the working knowledge and CTE leadership capacity that I have gained over the years can be attributed to the many opportunities provided through my belonging to, and participating in, ACTE at both the state and national levels.

Just belonging to the national ACTE organization provides many benefits in itself; one is a subscription to Techniques magazine, which has kept me updated on the latest topics and trends in CTE, a must for any CTE educator, whether a classroom teacher or administrator. Attending the national conference, ACTE's Career Tech VISION, has provided me with the opportunity to see CTE on the national level and gain a broader perspective of it. The examples and best practices of how CTE is working across the nation have given me information that I can put to work right away in my own work and practice.

Another opportunity that was provided to me was serving as the secretary, and then president, for California ACTE (CACTE), our state association. Through these experiences, I was able to meet and work with other CTE educators throughout the state, growing my network of colleagues. Not only have the members of this network served as my informal mentors along the way, but many of them have also become friends that I can count on as my "go-to" people when needing to address specific CTE issues in my current role at the state level.

Perhaps the greatest benefit of all has been the fact that someone else saw the value in ACTE and shared it with me, so that I could in turn share it with others. So, now that I have shared it with you, I hope that you too will find the benefits and value in belonging to a professional organization such as ACTE, and share it with others in the field.

Our second toolbox reflection comes from a diesel mechanics teacher in Pennsylvania who compares his entry into the field of education with entering a "strange new land." He likens his association to his trade group as a grounding of sorts, and a way for him to help his students visualize their futures:

I remember the morning fog that was dark and damp almost 20 years ago as I started my journey to a land that was most foreign to me. Leaving behind friends and surroundings made my one-way journey even bleaker. Attempting to convince myself that I had set out for all the right reasons only added to my fears as my journey departed into the abyss of the un-

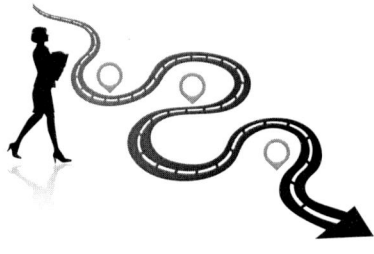

known. The inhabitants of this land spoke words that I was unfamiliar with and wore strange attire, quite different from my familiar uniform.

Of course, my "journey" above was a metaphor for my transition from technician to teacher. Coming into educa-tion from the world of work can feel as strange and fearful as sailing to an un-

known island. And as time goes by, one can begin to feel quite isolated, because few in school can offer assistance with non-educational dilemmas such as tool management, parts control, repair orders, diagnostic equip-ment, and much more. You have so much to do; sometimes it can feel as if the walls are closing in on you.

Comfort and security comes from being around people like yourself. My road to comfort and security began by involving myself with people in the transportation industry. There, I felt safe and understood the lan-guage, and I found others who were similarly searching for help and assis-tance. Uniting with an organization called Technology and Maintenance Council (TMC, see http://www.trucking.org/Technology_Council.aspx) in 2003 provided me with a connection to teachers like me, service man-agers, and technicians who were all struggling with similar issues. Com-municating with them, I found that the new skills in people management I had learned in my transition to education actually put me in a better position to solve some of these issues than other people. Reaching out to other professionals who were struggling in their day-to-day operations al-lowed me to gain a broader sense of the need to not only help my students and myself, but to also help the future generations of technicians who will all be embarking on their own journeys.

Involvement with industry groups (related to transportation) through social media sites, such as LinkedIn, provided me with new perspectives on the constant evolution of my field, and the necessity to evolve with new technologies. Coming to education "cold turkey" with no college back-ground is frightful, to say the least. Sometimes you and your program may feel isolated, as if on a deserted island, but trade associations like the TMC can be your Coast Guard, patrolling vigilantly, always ready to make the rescue.

Trying to go it alone in your program can mean you are depriving your students of important resources. These students look to you to be their eyes gazing into their future in your industry. Involvement in organizations like TMC not only opens your eyes, but, by disseminating newfound knowledge and resources to your students, also helps you to greatly increase their likelihood for success.

Our third and final entry comes from an administrator in Ohio and she talks about the benefits of having her school participate in an Educational Institution Membership with ACTE:

"I've been lucky," as one of my favorite songs starts. I've had the opportunity to work as an administrator in several comprehensive districts and a very large career-technical district. While many functions were similar, what a difference! The life experiences and educational backgrounds of employees at career centers are much more diverse. The lens through which they look is different. There is a common core belief of "whatever it takes," so that each and every learner is successful.

The transition from a comprehensive district to a career center has its challenges. There's a new set of educational terminology to learn. That hasn't changed in education. The abbreviations and acronyms ... NCCER, HOSA, CTSO, HSTW, ACTE ...you get the picture. I needed a glossary.

State and national membership in ACTE is a critical tool and resource for any career technical educator, and especially for a career technical administrator. The association is the best single source of research on best practice for instruction, career development, work-based learning, assessment, and employment trends nationally and globally. As institutional members, teachers have access to the experts in the field. We can therefore put their research into practice to ensure our students are prepared for careers, college and life—nothing is more important!

To be an effective administrator, one must be aware of our influence on local, state, and federal legislators in passing legislative policy and funding to ensure our students are prepared to compete globally in the workforce. ACTE plays an active role in seeking input from its membership, providing critical information and current data to the field as we work with legislators to benefit our students, schools, and communities. ACTE has developed, and maintains, a network of researchers and analytics to assist teachers in data-driven conversations and decisions.

Probably the most beneficial benefit of membership, is the professional networking provided from across the country to identify innovative practices and solutions to meet the needs of our employers and communities. ACTE allows its members to interact in multiple formats, serving as a leading source of information on career education and data-supported successes, as well as innovative solutions to meet the workforce needs of communities of today and the future.

KEY LEARNINGS:

1. Becoming a CTE professional takes commitment.
2. Commitment involves time, talent, and participation.
3. It is critical that you develop a trusted professional network.
4. Actively seek opportunities for leadership and professional learning.
5. Consider the value of professional journals, both electronic and print-based.
6. Join ACTE and tell your peers to do the same!
7. Reflect on how you can keep your technical expertise current.
8. Stretch your thinking, and get comfortable being uncomfortable.

RELATED CONTENT THAT MAY BE OF INTEREST:

Advance CTE. (2016). State Leaders *Connecting Learning to Work*. https://www.careertech.org/.

Association for Career and Technical Education (ACTE). (2016). Connecting Education and Careers. Available at www.acteonline.org/join.

Baden-Powell, R. (1941). AZ Quotes. Available at http://www.az-quotes.com/author/759-Robert_Baden_Powell.

Cole, B., Foster, J.C., Foster, P. & McNally, K. (2014). *Your First Year in CTE: 10 things to know*. Alexandria, VA: ACTE.

Foster, J.C., Foster, P., Hornberger, C. & McNally, K. (2015). *Your First Year in CTE: 10 More Things to Know.* Alexandria, VA: ACTE.

California Center for College and Career. (2010). Stanford, CA: Author. Available at https://edpolicy.stanford.edu/news/articles/597.

Lakein, A. (1989). *How to Get Control of Your Time and Your Life*. Signet Books. New York: New York.

Pennsylvania Association of Career and Technical Administrators (PACTA). (2016). Resources. Available at http://www.pacareertech.org/resources/categories.

Post, P. (2014, August 17). Traits that convey character also define a professional. *Boston Globe, Business Section*. Available at https://www.bostonglobe.com/business/2014/08/16/just-what-does-mean-professional/MTlZfzUhw4cDphH6E99LIO/story.html.

Zetlin, M. (2014, December). 9 Secrets to Effective Networking, Even If You're a Nerd. *Inc.* Available at http://www.inc.com/minda-zetlin/9-secrets-to-effective-networking-even-if-you-re-a-nerd.html.

chapter III

BIG Picture Ideas

Connections That Count

Most of us have heard the phrase "drinking from a fire hydrant." If you haven't, it's a metaphor that means that you are receiving so much that you can't possibly take it all in. Many of you reading this book knew almost everything about your technical specialty, but now that you have transitioned into CTE, you almost feel like you have to start over again! Many initiatives are occurring in the field of general education. What we'll do in this chapter is focus on some important CTE-related initiatives, along with some context and history. As an educator, you know that using context not only provides information, but it also helps you retain the content! So, let's get started.

Outgrowths From Legislation

In Chapter I, the Smith Hughes Act (2016) was mentioned, but without much context. Back in 1917, this legislation, formally called the National Vocational Education Act, provided for a trade or vocational education for those who were preparing to enter careers in agriculture or industry The legislation was intended for individuals who society assumed would not be attending college. Although this piece of legislation was directed toward vocational agriculture, trade and industrial education and home economics, it set a precedent for future legislation that supported CTE as it exists today.

As the American economy changed, the direction of legislation associated with CTE broadened beyond agriculture. For example, after World War II, the focus was placed upon getting individuals (both male and female) into the world of work, but still the target was students who were not planning on attending post-secondary education. Early Perkins legislation (1984) provided federal money for vocational education targeted toward helping disadvantaged and handicapped students (again, students who, it was presumed, would most likely not be attending college.)

As the technical requirements of the different occupational areas grew, the need for post-secondary CTE education grew as well. Later versions of Perkins legislation (Perkins II, 1990; Perkins III, 1998) focused on ways to better connect secondary and post-secondary CTE education. A major philosophical shift in CTE occurred with the enactment of Perkins II (1990); this legislation addressed the need to integrate academic and vocational studies. The rationale was to strengthen the U.S. workforce preparation system to maintain global competitiveness (Threeton, 2007).

One example of this was "Tech Prep," the basis of which was an articulation agreement between institutions on a sequence of secondary vocational courses that aligned with the first two years of college, primarily a community or technical college. In addition, integration of academic content into vocational courses was included in an attempt to create more rigorous programs (U.S. Department of Education, 2004). This was a major shift of thinking in CTE. No longer were high-school CTE students seen as only going directly into the world of work after high school; they were seen as students who needed additional technical education due to the increasing complexity of that work.

Perkins III continued this focus and increased accountability for vocational student performance. More recent Perkins legislation (Perkins IV, 2006) continued to emphasize alignment of curriculum and articulation of secondary and post-secondary education; this authorization of Perkins legislation was also better aligned with the Elementary and Secondary Education Act, or ESEA, better known at the time as No Child Left Behind.

Perkins IV officially changed the name "vocational education" to "career technical education." In addition, there was an emphasis on programs of study spanning secondary and postsecondary education and increased accountability. The more seamless the transition between secondary and post-secondary education, the more beneficial it is for students. Multiple initiatives are being utilized that enhance this transition, which we briefly describe below::

- **Integration of CTE and required classes:** Since Perkins III, there has been an ongoing effort in CTE to show the amount of theoretical knowledge that can be taught in a CTE program or  pathway. Additionally, since this academic knowledge tends to be contextualized, it is argued that students tend to learn and retain it better. An example of this is the Pythagorean Theorem, which is a geometry concept regarding the lengths of the sides of a right triangle. Within a number of CTE programs, this academic knowledge can be used to square a frame or wall, to lay out a foundation, or to establish a square grid of some type. In a number of states, the academic standards are being cross-walked (or identified) within the CTE program standards. The integration of CTE and academics is most often the responsibility of the teacher.

- **College credit for credentials:** A current trend in both secondary and post-secondary schools is the awarding of credit if a student has successfully acquired some sort of an industry-driven credential. An example of this can be found with regard to NOCTI assessments. If a student meets or exceeds the predetermined score, a number of credits are recommended that can be used in over 1500 cooperating colleges and universities (NCCRS, 2016).

- **Credit for prior learning:** A growing number of colleges and universities have developed systems to award credit, typically for adult students, for learning that has taken place on the job. By doing this, these institutions are recognizing that learning takes place in many settings outside of a typical learning environment. Students who receive college credit this way tend to complete their degrees more often than those who do not have this option, as they are closer to graduation (Lakin, Nellum, Seymour, & Crandall, 2015).

- **Dual enrollment:** This program allows students, not exclusively CTE students, to obtain college credit while still in a high school (U.S. Department of Education, 2004). In some schools, a local college or university sends a teacher to dual-enrollment high schools or high school students take courses on a postsecondary campus. In other situations, the existing high school teacher has the credentials required by the college or university to deliver the courses for which the students will receive dual credit. It is quite evident that this is beneficial to high school students and enables them to get a jump-start on their postsecondary education.

- **Program of Study:** Usually referred to as POS, a program of study is a comprehensive, structured approach for delivering academic and career and technical education to prepare students for postsecondary education and career success. The Carl D. Perkins Career and Technical Education Act of 2006 (Perkins IV) requires that all eligible providers offer at least one program of study that:
  - Incorporates secondary education and postsecondary education elements;
  - Includes coherent and rigorous content aligned with challenging academic standards and relevant career and technical content in a coordinated, non-duplicative progression of courses that align secondary to postsecondary education;
  - May include opportunity for secondary education students to gain postsecondary education credits through dual or concurrent enrollment programs or other means; and
  - Leads to an industry-recognized credential or certificate at the postsecondary level or an associate or baccalaureate degree.

Grassroots Initiatives

Recent demands by employers for higher and more specialized skillsets has increased the need for schools and students to achieve higher levels of academic and technical knowledge. Advancements in technology and global competition have resulted in greater demands for highly skilled workers and the ability to continue to learn. Enter "lifelong learning."

Former Secretary of Education, Arne Duncan, stated in his comments regarding release of the "Pathway to Prosperity" report (2011):

"The mission of CTE has to change. It can no longer be about earning a diploma and landing a job after high school. The goal of CTE 2.0 should be that students earn a post-secondary degree or an industry-recognized certification—and land a job that leads to a successful career." (p. 3)

The Harvard Graduate School of Education and Jobs for the Future has created a Pathways to Prosperity Network to increase high school completion and credit attainment so students can obtain high-demand, high-wage occupations. Harvard Graduate School of Education and Jobs for the Future works with a network of states to improve the organizational structure of educational programs (Pathways to Prosperity State Network, 2014).

Post-secondary education (formal or informal) has become a requirement for many technical occupations. Students may be exposed to a number of CTE occupations at the secondary level, but typically focus their educational efforts at the post-secondary level, as more than sixty percent of today's jobs require some post-secondary education and training (Carnevale, 2016). Additionally, as the technical requirements in many occupational areas increase, it becomes more challenging to teach all these at the secondary level. It should be noted that the more alignment between the secondary and post-secondary level institutions, the more beneficial it is for students in transitioning between the two because there will be less content and curriculum duplication.

CTE schools and community and technical colleges began to use third-party industry and industry recognized credentials (e.g. NOCTI) to address local or state requirements. The additional benefit of these assessments is the opportunity it provides students to be awarded college credits and/or advanced standing in associate and baccalaureate degree programs.

Evaluation and Accountability

"Accountability" is a major buzzword in the educational world today. Under Perkins, states have had to comply with accountability reporting on a series of measures for a number of years. As a CTE teacher, you should be aware of the many different stakeholders for which you and your CTE program/pathway need to be accountable. These include people from business and industry, state or national accrediting agencies, parents and students, and local school boards or boards of control.

It is necessary to show business and industry employers that there is an ongoing effort to ensure that the CTE program/pathway is staying current with the related field. One way to ensure this is through the use of an occupational advisory board (Foster, Foster, Hornberger & McNally, 2015) that will oversee and provide input on the CTE curriculum and equipment, while providing general oversight of the CTE program/pathway.

For state and national accrediting agencies, it is necessary to demonstrate that what is being taught in a CTE program/pathway aligns with program approval at the state or level. It is also is necessary to ensure the CTE teacher has, or is obtaining, the necessary credentials from the appropriate credentialing bodies.

Parents have a need to know that education is a good fit for their child's future educational and/or work-based pursuits. Students should have the same information as the parents. Effort needs to be made to keep the parents apprised of how curriculum and equipment within CTE program/pathways are constantly being evaluated and updated as needed.

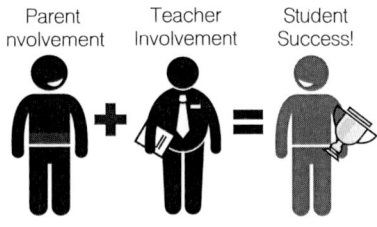

Parent Involvement + Teacher Involvement = Student Success!

The local school board or board of control also needs to have evidence that what is being taught in a CTE program/pathway meets the requirements of the state or national accrediting agency. Much of what is used to show accountability to state and national accrediting bodies can be used to demonstrate accountability to these boards.

Tools For Your Toolbox

Our first entry in the *Tools* section for this chapter comes from Kansas. It demonstrates how big-picture ideas can be rolled into state initiatives, in this case, ideas like transitioning and credentialing:

> In Kansas, legislation was passed to encourage secondary and post-secondary schools to work more closely together to stimulate growth in CTE. Legislators and educators realized that the Kansas workforce was increasingly demanding more highly technical and skilled workers, and the bill was aimed at meeting these demands. The four financial aspects included:
>
> - *Tuition reimbursement* for high school students enrolled in college-level CTE courses
> - Incentivizing high school students graduating with industry-recognized certifications that lead directly to high-demand occupations through a certification incentive program
> - *Transportation reimbursement* to school districts transporting high school students off-campus to complete college-level CTE coursework, and
> - *A CTE marketing campaign* to promote the positive impact of CTE on education and the workforce.

Our second entry comes to us from the state of Pennsylvania and includes the state-approved career education and work standards. The standards and competencies are presented below and serve as a great starting point for those schools and states that may not have policies in place regarding employability skills:

Career Awareness and Preparation

- Relate careers to individual interests, abilities, and aptitudes.
- Analyze career options based on personal interests, abilities, aptitudes, achievements, and goals.
- Analyze how the changing roles of individuals in the workplace relate to new opportunities within career choices.
- Evaluate school-based opportunities for career awareness/preparation.
- Justify the selection of a career.
- Analyze the relationship between career choices and career-preparation opportunities.
- Assess the implementation of the individualized career plan through the ongoing development of the career portfolio.
- Review personal high school plan against current personal career goals and select post-secondary opportunities based upon personal career interests.

Career Acquisition (Getting a Job)

- Apply effective speaking and listening skills used in a job interview.
- Apply research skills in searching for a job.
- Emphasis upon creating comprehensive job applications and on writing letters of appreciation after interview.
- Analyze, revise, and apply an individualized career portfolio to chosen career path.
- Demonstrate the application of essential workplace skills/knowledge in the career acquisition process.

Career Retention and Advancement

- Evaluate personal attitudes and work habits that support career retention and advancement.
- Evaluate team member roles to describe and illustrate active listening techniques.
- Evaluate conflict-resolution skills as they relate to the workplace.
- Develop a personal budget based on career choice.
- Evaluate time-management strategies and their application to both personal and work situations.

- Evaluate strategies for career retention and advancement in response to the changing global workplace.
- Evaluate the impact of lifelong learning on career retention and advancement.

Entrepreneurship

- Analyze entrepreneurship as it relates to personal career goals and corporate opportunities.
- Analyze entrepreneurship as it relates to personal character traits.
- Develop a business plan for an entrepreneurial concept of personal interest and identify available resources.

Our final resource comes from a seasoned electronics teacher in North Carolina who discusses his "four pillars." These four pillars incorporate the kind of big picture ideas this chapter is about: articulation, for example. We hope this teacher's reflection helps you to think about the benefits of your program and how you might enhance them:

There are four pillars that support a highly successful electronics program, and each serves a purpose in ensuring that my completers are workforce ready, motivated, and proficient in the trade. These four pillars not only serve to improve outcomes and motivate students to work harder in the classroom and lab setting, but also help the parents and general public to recognize the value of the program and the impact it can have on students.

The first foundation is, of course, a curriculum aligned with the objectives outlined in the Standard Course of Study. In North Carolina, we align to vendor-provided Industry Certifications, which makes the task of developing a program much easier. Parents and the general public rarely see any direct evidence of this component, so it is essential to have the other three pillars.

The second pillar is industry certifications. My students know from day one of the class that if they apply themselves and work hard to attain the skills and competencies, they can earn an ETA (Electronics Technicians Association) certification in electronics. This is a great motivational tool for many students who otherwise might attempt to just coast through the course. Since the state pays for these tests, it is simple to challenge students early in the year with, "Why not attempt this? You have nothing to lose." Yearly, my program generates over 20 ETA-certified students, and the pride they take in this achievement sets an example for following classes. This also serves to show these young people that they can learn and achieve recognition in the field. We share these successes with the public via the school website, local media, and the school system's website.

A third important pillar that demonstrates the benefits of the program is the articulation agreement we have with a local college. Students who successfully complete two semesters of the curriculum and attain a proficiency score on the final exam can opt out of a 5-credit-hour class at the local college. This not only provides an advantage to those students pursuing a post-secondary education, but it also saves them and their parents' money.

The final pillar consists of an active CTSO chapter in which students have the opportunity to compete in the program area. These competitions offer students several benefits above and beyond the positive "press" they get from winning awards. Students get to compete using the skills and knowledge that they have gained, and also have the opportunity to network with business and industry professionals. This and other soft skills help students prepare not only for the technical aspects of our trade, but also for some of the interpersonal skills required for success in any field.

KEY LEARNINGS:

1. Legislation helps drive new ideas.
2. CTE has benefited from the evolution of legislation.
3. Legislation shifts with the needs of society.
4. CTE provides context for academic classroom-based learning.
5. College credit for technical competence is a "big idea."
6. Avoiding duplication of content is critical.
7. Secondary to post-secondary articulation benefits everyone.
8. Accountability comes in all shapes and sizes.

RELATED CONTENT THAT MAY BE OF INTEREST:

Brookings Institution. (2013). The Hidden STEM Economy. Retrieved from http://www.brookings.edu/research/interactives/2013/the-hidden-stem-economy.

Carl D. Perkins Career and Technical Education Act of 2006 (Perkins IV). (Public Law 109-270).

Carl D. Perkins Career and Technical Education Act of 1998 (Perkins III). (Public Law 105-332).

Carl D. Perkins Career and Technical Education Act of 1990 (Perkins II). (Public Law 101-392).

Carl D. Perkins Vocational Education Act of 1984. (Public Law 98-524).

Carnevale, A. (2016, May 31). *Credentials and Competencies: Demonstrating The Economic Value of Post-secondary Education*. Parchment Summit on Innovating Academic Credentials. Available at https://cew.georgetown.edu/publications/journals-articles/

Duncan, A. (2011, February 2). *The New CTE: Secretary Duncan's Prepared Remarks at the Release of the "Pathways to Prosperity" Report.* Retrieved from http://www.ed.gov/news/speeches/new-cte-secretary-duncans-remarks-career-and-technical-education.

Foster, J.C., Foster, P., Hornberger, C., & McNally, K. (2015). Chapter IX, Connecting with Occupational Advisory Committees. *In Your First Year in CTE: 10 more things to know.* Alexandria, VA: ACTE

Industrial Maintenance and Plant Operation. (2015, June). Jobs Report 2015. *IMPO*. Available at www.impomag.com.

Klein-Collins, R. (2010). *Fueling the Race to Post-secondary Success: A 48-Institution Study of Prior Learning Assessment and Adult Student Outcomes.* Chicago, IL: Council for Adult and Experiential Learning. Available at http://cdn2.hubspot.net/hubfs/617695/premium_content_resources/pla/PDF/PLA_Fueling-the-Race.pdf.

Lakin, M., Nellum, D., Seymour, C. & Crandall, J. (2015). *Credit for Prior Learning: Charting Institutional Practice for Sustainability.* Washington, DC: American Council on Education. Available at https://www.acenet.edu/news-room/Documents/Credit-for-Prior-Learning-Charting-Institutional-Practice-for-Sustainability.pdf.

National College Credit Recommendation Service (NCCRS). (2016). *Cooperating Colleges and Universities.* Available at http://www.nationalccrs.org/organizations/nocti-and-nocti-business.

Pathways to Prosperity State Network. (2014, June). *State Progress Report, 2012-2014.* Jobs for the Future: Boston, MA. ED561260.

RELATED CONTENT THAT MAY BE OF INTEREST, continued:

Pennsylvania Department of Education. (2016). Pennsylvania Academic Standards Crosswalk, Grade 11. Available at http://www.education.pa.gov/K-12/PACareerStandards/Curriculum/Pages/Crosswalks.aspx#tab-1.

Schwartz, R. B. (2014, Fall). The Pursuit of Pathways: Combining rigorous academics with career training. *American Educator*, pp 24-29, 41.

Shumer, R., & Digby, C. (2012, January). The future of CTE: Programs of study. *Techniques: Connecting Education and Careers*, 87(1) pp. 36-39. EJ976604.

Smith-Hughes Act. (2016). In *Encyclopædia Britannica*. Retrieved from https://www.britannica.com/topic/Smith-Hughes-Act.

Stipanovic, N., Shumer, R., & Stringfield, S. (2012). Lessons learned from highly implemented programs of study, *Techniques: Connecting Education and Careers*, 87(1) 21-23. EJ976600.

Threeton, M.D. (2007, Spring). The Carl D. Perkins Career and Technical Education (CTE) Act of 2006 and the Roles and Responsibilities of CTE Teachers and Faculty Members. *Journal of Industrial Teacher Education*, 44(1). Available at http://scholar.lib.vt.edu/ejournals/JITE/v44n1/threeton.html.

U.S. Department of Education, Office of the Under Secretary, Policy and Program Studies Service. (2004). *National Assessment of Vocational Education: Final Report to Congress*, Washington, D.C.: Author.

Wells, A. (2014). Why The Manufacturing Skills Gap Is Serious. *Manufacturing Net*. Available at http://www.manufacturing.net/blog/2014/06/why-manufacturing-skills-gap-serious.

chapter IV

Visibility in Your Community

Can You See Me Now?

Educators: People We Look Up To

Have you ever had the feeling while shopping that someone (possible someone younger) is taking a second glance at you as the two of you pass by each other in the aisles? Maybe that individual will even approach you and say something like, "Hey, aren't you Mr. Neuteach?" This is a pretty common experience for CTE teachers. The conversation will typically go like this:

"Yes, I'm Mr. Neuteach."

"Hi, Mr. Neuteach. You might not remember me, but I'm Sam Smith and I was in your class in 2010."

"Yes, I remember you, Sam. What have you been up to?"

"Well, you remember that internship you helped me find in 2009?"

"Yes, I do remember."

"Well that experience, combined with the important skills that you helped me to learn over three years, led to an even better opportunity at Best Manufacturing Co."

"Wow, Sam, that's great! I'm glad I was able to help!"

"Mr. Neuteach, I always wanted to say thank you, so I'm really glad we were both shopping this evening!"

Needless to say, it takes only one experience like this early in your career, and you are hooked on one of the intangible benefits of teaching in a CTE program for life.

One of the most important gifts anyone can receive from another person is respect. As a CTE teacher, you have many opportunities to earn that respect with the students you guide. After all, you have the opportunity to spend greater amounts of time with these students than do many of your educational peers. You have an  opportunity to form a relationship based on trust and a shared interest in an area of technical expertise. We discussed this relationship a little bit in *Your First Year in CTE: 10 Things to Know* Chapter V (Cole, 2014). However, that discussion was more about establishing new relationships. This chapter is about what you can and should do to maintain those relationships.

Let's think for a minute about the value of continually developing that respect as you continue your teaching career. Good teachers should convey four key beliefs to their students (Tough, 2016):

FOUR BELIEFS

1. I belong in the CTE community,
2. My ability and competence grow with my effort,
3. I can succeed at this, and
4. This work has value for me.

Giving students a sense of belonging and success is key. In addition to the intrinsic benefits you receive from knowing that you helped someone, it can help further your career as a CTE teacher.

Remember, CTE is an elective; students have to want to participate in it. Whatever the technical content area you teach, it is something that you love. You want others to love it too, but those others may not even be aware of the opportunity. As a CTE educator your job is not only to teach technical content; it's also about awareness of the social and behavioral skills students need to succeed (Salemi, 2016).

In many cases, a student's first exposure to technical content is through you! Because you represent your particular industry specialty, people have to form a positive mental connection between that industry and you. You can't wear a sandwich board (an old marketing ploy) every time you are out in public, so forming positive relationships through word of mouth via your classroom is one of your most effective means of becoming a professional and respected leader (Green, 2013).

When you think about it, students in your class really know you best. They quickly get a sense of your background and your technical experience. As you teach, it's important that you share your professional experiences. This sharing must be sincere and genuine and must teach students something that will reinforce their existing skillset. These kinds of examples are not only a good instructional technique, but they also make you a more interesting individual, one with whom people want to associate. Students will remember those stories and tell other students about them. That connects directly to that word-of-mouth advertising we were talking about.

GOOD JOB!

Some teachers take the time to recognize past graduates on their personal media sites or on bulletin boards. This shows that people who graduate from those programs are successful. It also shows that the teacher makes the effort to proudly recognize his or her students. Lastly, it helps establish the teacher as a professional, a leader in the field, and one with whom students want to be associated.

Name five people whom you would consider a major influence in your life. Look over this list and think what it was about these people did that had an impact on you.

The people you list tend to be those who valued you and invested time with you to show they cared. Therefore, educators need to remember that when a CTE teacher impacts students' lives, he or she also impacts their futures. When individuals are positively impacted by another person, they are more likely to pay it forward with similar positive acts. Can you think of a better investment to make in our society?

The Importance of Visibility in Education

We've discussed teachers who utilize their skills and knowledge as leaders in the classroom. In that environment, they have a longer period of time to get to know their students and for their students to get to know them. In CTE classrooms, this exposure can be as long as four years. During the course of a year, the time spent with a single cohort of students might be as high as 360 hours. From what we've seen nationally, the average time a CTE teacher spends with his or her students is probably about 480 hours over the years of the program. That's a lot of time to make an impression and be visible with the population of students you teach.

What about becoming more visible in the education institution in which you work? Think about the contact time that you may have had with educators in your building. Let's assume that you have had three years of experience. Compare the total time you have spent with the staff as a whole to the time you've spent with your students. Big difference, right? So transforming yourself into a visible educational leader in this environment will force you to be much more aggressive. You'll want to volunteer for school leadership positions and show a can-do attitude. Share your student successes with other faculty members and ask about their successful students.

You might consider exchanging teaching strategies with other teachers and engaging them in discussions on what works. You can also organize small discussion groups of teachers to meet and talk about ways to become more effective with students. Exchanging views about your profession with peers as part of a professional community is the best way to begin to establish your engagement and leadership as an educator.

For those CTE teachers who work in schools with high concentrations of CTE students, an obvious choice to be more visible to a larger population would be to consider becoming an advisor to one of the many Career Technical Student Organizations (CTSOs), as discussed in *Your First Year in CTE: 10 MORE Things to Know*, Chapter IV (Foster, 2015). CTSOs like Future Farmers of America (FFA), Future Business Leaders of America (FBLA), and SkillsUSA are just a few of the student organizations with which you could help (U.S. Department of Education, 2016). Their websites have information about what serving as an advisor in a CTSO is all about, or you can simply ask your supervisor or the existing advisor if the organization can use an extra pair of hands. Maybe your school doesn't have a CTSO, or maybe they had one and its membership faltered. What an opportunity and a challenge it would be for you to establish a new program or revive one!

Think about other things that occur in the school community, especially if you are in a comprehensive school, which offers both technical and academic classes. Maybe this school has athletic teams, which provide great opportunities for someone who has an interest in coaching or athletic training. If there is a theater club, think about opportunities to help in make-up or set design. Remember that you represent your particular technical specialty; as more people get to know you, they will get to know your program too!

Schools are typically community hubs, and they often offer opportunities to volunteer in areas outside your field of technical expertise.

COMMUNITY HUB

Opportunities abound for providing assistance to charitable groups, food drives, and fundraisers for national efforts whether fighting a disease or assisting with relief efforts after a national disaster. These are not only opportunities to be visible, but also opportunities to show leadership and to help others.

The Importance of Visibility in Your Community

So far we have discussed exposure time related to your visibility. In your classroom, you can create opportunities to demonstrate a variety of educational leadership skills. Within your school community, demonstrating that you, as an administrator, are committed to your school and its overall goals is about responding to the needs of others and making suggestions for improvements. Of course, in the community that you live in, you'll want to be seen as a good citizen, but you'll also want to be seen as a positive representative of the educational community (i.e. visible). Because you have specialized content knowledge and skills, you should consider how you might use those to be most helpful, as well as to become a more visible community participant.

Fill The Gap!

How do CTE educators and their students benefit when they connect with their community, and why is that beneficial to all involved? As Baby Boomers continue to retire, many industry partners face looming local and national crises to fill the labor gap of this graying workforce (Walker, 2012). This is a large contributing factor for what the media has labeled a "skills gap". This "skills gap" is generally recognized as a shortage of skilled workers when compared to employers needs. CTE educators can contribute to lessening this gap in their communities by helping to create a pipeline of qualified workers when they work closely with local employers. They can better prepare the next generation of workers through student apprenticeship programs, paid or unpaid internships, co-op student programs, job shadowing, guest speakers, mentoring, mock job interviews, field trips, community fundraisers, and obtaining national certifications during high school or post-secondary programs, among other opportunities.

CTE educators can also engage their local businesses and industries by discussing workplace skill requirements with their representatives, serving on advisory committees, recommending students for job placements, inviting employers to make presentations to students in class, and arranging for students to visit employer work sites (Pawlowski, 2016). Sometimes local business and industry organizations may be able to provide equipment/funds to purchase equipment for CTE school lab facilities. They may also be able to offer professional development and services to teachers and students. It should be a win-win for all involved.

CTE educators can form positive relationships with community orga-  nizations by becoming involved with the local Chamber of Commerce or Rotary Club, serving as church committee members, demonstrating leadership as scout leaders or assistants, or becoming active in trade groups. If your field relates to using small hand tools and measuring devices, for example, you could demonstrate leadership by volunteering to help Cub Scouts with a birdhouse construction project.

Regardless of your occupational specialty, you can encourage parents and prospective middle school students to explore careers in your spe-  cialty by teaching in summer career camps. Typically, middle school students explore careers by spending one to two weeks during the summer engaging in "high-touch" learning activities related to their interests. Many schools encourage parents to shadow their child on the first day of career camp. Working at one of these camps is an excellent way for you to increase your community engagement and to build interest in CTE and your program.

Whichever community organization you choose to participate in, do it for the community, your school, your students, but also for yourself. Actively seeking opportunities to help others demonstrates your initiative. You will most likely find that any of these opportunities are well worth your time and effort.

Tools For Your Toolbox

The first entry in the *Tools* section for this chapter comes from a collision repair program in Kansas. It demonstrates how relationships and personal commitment can result in creative solutions that benefit your community and raise the visibility of your program. The program discussed below began as a result of a discussion among local advisory council members:

> One evening we were brainstorming about new methods to engage the students with our industry outside of the normal class time. Someone suggested that we look into some form of working on cars for charity. I had been involved with the National Auto Body Council (NABC) in the past

as a business owner. I knew that NABC had a charitable program called "Recycled Rides." I had actually submitted an application to NABC to be one of the test locations for the pilot program to bring Recycled Rides into our school. During the discussion, one of our members, a shop manager at a dealership collision repair facility, offered up an idea. The manager had a car in the shop currently that the owner had decided not to repair, and the owner was willing to donate the vehicle to a charity.

We brought the vehicle to our location. The NABC Executive Director happened to be in town for a meeting, and we were able to get him to visit our school. While touring our classroom, he saw the car and commented that we should be part of the NABC Recycled Rides for Schools. I mentioned that we had applied for one of the pilot spots but did not make the cut. By the end of the day, we were able to reverse that decision, and we received approval for a pilot spot! Our administration was positive and very supportive of the project.

In September of 2011, we had a kick-off meeting with local businesses to garner interest in donation of parts, supplies and labor. We scheduled and held a marathon weekend to repair our first vehicle, and in November 2011, we gifted that vehicle. Since that time, we have gifted 16 vehicles. It has been a very positive program; we even have past graduates, now working in the industry, who come back to help at our repair-a-thons. It has been a good way to bring industry technicians and support staff together with students looking for careers in the automotive field.

In some cases, the event has the added benefit of becoming a live job interview for our students. After the repairs, we have had local shops call and ask about a particular student who they may have worked with during the repair-a-thon; they want to talk to them about job shadowing or on-the-job training. Some students have received their current jobs due to the interaction they had with shop personnel while working side by side on the "Recycled Rides" vehicles.

The majority of the work is done on weekends and evenings. We have shop technicians, managers, estimators, insurance adjusters, parts vendors, service vendors such as paint-less dent repair people, and other community volunteers that come in and work with—and encourage—our students. Other programs on campus have gotten involved with us too, including our culinary program, which helps to supply meals during our workdays, and our graphic arts program, which handles our publicity material and donor appreciation efforts. Our administration and staff also do a lot of our behind-the-scenes work. Our local United Way chairs the committee that oversees the nominations for recipients of the "Recycled Rides," and they include two or three student ambassadors of the program to help make the final selection.

Our vehicle giftings are widely attended too, and we have had three events at the state capitol with the governor and other dignitaries in attendance. Because of the publicity that we receive from these giftings, we periodically receive calls from community members also wanting to donate vehicles. Who could have predicted that a little discussion would have the ability to make our program so visible in our state!

We asked an executive chef, turned CTE teacher, why he thinks visibility is important, and the kinds of things he does to make his classroom vibrant in central Pennsylvania:

Why would I want community visibility for me and my program? All professional industries build their businesses on personal relationships that tie themselves to their community and surroundings. This type of networking is essential to building a good CTE program; it will help promote good citizenship while exposing your students to great educational experiences. As you build your CTE program, you will soon realize that to have a successful program you need to offer a variety of educational experiences to give your students a well-rounded environment. As you have learned, sharing these varied experiences provides a learning opportunity that makes it more personal for the student. These personal experiences also allow your students to see their skills being put to use outside the classroom as they start to apply those skills to the real world. This will help your students transition from the classroom to the world of work more seamlessly.

To have a successful program, you will need to offer experiences that cannot be replicated within the limited walls of your classroom. Take that step out of your classroom and into the world and share the talents and gifts of your program and your students. Utilize those talents and turn your community needs into a great teaching experience.

Before taking on any community project or out-of-the-classroom experiences, I use these simple questions to see if this is something that is beneficial to both the program and my students.

1. Is it an educational opportunity that aligns with the program's objectives?
2. Does it promote the students and program in a positive light?
3. Does the experience cut into or take away from the program curriculum?
4. Is the event paid for by the event itself, so that it doesn't take away from limited instructional resources?

Here are a few of the opportunities which we have challenged our program to take advantage of:

1. **The American Heart Association** does numerous fundraising events. Our area hosts an annual "Heart Ball," a gala V.I.P. dinner at a local country club that raises money to support our local American Heart Association chapter.

   We were asked by the association if our pastry arts program would like to create the desserts for the event. My students now plan, create and plate the desserts off-school property. The students get to work in another commercial kitchen and with the club's staff. They are recognized at the dinner and on the menu, giving the program community visibility and helping to raise funds for a great cause.

2. **American Culinary Federation Education Foundation (ACFEF)** holds two national board meetings each year. We hosted one of their board meetings, and were the first secondary program to host this event. The students prepared all the breaks and meals for the event, which was hosted at our school. This gave our program and school quite a bit of national visibility within the culinary community.

3. **Summer Cooking Schools** offers another unique opportunity. Recently, our school was approached by our local Intermediate Unit about creating a summer cooking school program for displaced workers. This was a two-week intense hands-on kitchen experience that ended with a job fair and employment for all students that graduated from the class. Our program helps students to address community and industry needs by sharing our knowledge, resources, and kitchens.

Because the area and world we live in is constantly changing, as educators we must also be willing to change. An event or opportunity you did one year may not work or exist the next. Be aware of your community and industry needs and always be willing to adapt.

An auto mechanics teacher in Vermont emphasized the importance of visibility as a professional educator through personal relationships:

In reflecting on the topic of visibility in one's community, I'm reminded of a quote by David F. Labaree in his paper, How Dewey Lost: The Victory of David Snedden and Social Efficiency in the Reform of American Education. "But the pedagogical progressives, with their focus primarily on teaching and learning in classrooms, had to rely on individual teachers to adopt their vision and implement it one class at a time. Not only were teachers in a weak organizational position to bring about the Deweyan vision, but they found themselves trapped within an organizational and curricular structure of schooling that was shaped by the administrative progressive vision of social efficiency."

Unfortunately, there are some who see CTE as simply job-specific training which provides human capital for business. That misconception needs to be corrected. As a CTE professional it's important to remember that every interaction you have with a student, parent, business leader, school board member, custodian, or even the person cutting your hair will leave that person with an impression not only of you, but also of the field you represent.

Having a few ideas to facilitate the discussion can be helpful. This takes preparation and some personal reflection as to what it is you're actually doing in your classroom. Many times when someone new finds out what I do for a living, they'll say something like, "Oh, you teach kids to fix cars." My typical response is, "... well, yes, students learn about various systems and components of the automobile, but we really use the car to teach broader academic content as it relates to the operation of the automobile." Sometimes I'll give an example of how Pascal's theory of hydraulics, which is often a component of a physics class, comes to life when associated with the hydraulic braking system of a modern automobile.

In addition to cultivating relationships on the local level, it's important to become affiliated with advocacy groups that share your vision and goals such as ACTE, NEA (National Education Association) and trade groups associated with your program of study. While in today's digital age Twitter, Facebook, and Snapchat can all be seen as a means of marketing, it is my opinion that you and your program will be better served by forming and cultivating personal relationships.

KEY LEARNINGS:

1. Respect is a gift you give to others.
2. Make others aware of CTE opportunities.
3. Student recognition demonstrates you care.
4. Look for opportunities to assist other educators.
5. Improve your profession.
6. Consider assisting in school-related extracurricular activities.
7. Contribute to the community in which you live.
8. Look for opportunities to shine.

RELATED CONTENT THAT MAY BE OF INTEREST:

ACTE. (2008, March). Career and Technical Education's Role in Workforce Readiness Credentials. *ACTE Issue Brief*. Available at www.acteonline.org.

Cole, B. (2014). Chapter V: Sometimes You Have to Build Fences. In Cole, B., Foster, J., Foster, P. & McNally, K., *Your First Year in CTE: Ten Things to Know*, pp. 32-37. Alexandria, VA: ACTE.

Green, A. (2013, July 22). What Does It Mean to Be Professional at Work? *U.S. News and World Report*, On Careers Blog. Available at http://money.usnews.com/money/blogs/outside-voices-careers/2013/07/22/what-does-it-mean-to-be-professional-at-work.

Pawlowski, B. (2016, March). Finding and Engaging Business Partners, *Techniques*, *91*(3), pp. 14-17. Available at www.acteonline.org.

Salemi, V. (2016, January 12). 4 Traits that a Hiring Manager Wants in a New Employee. *U.S. News and World Report*, On Careers Blog. Available at http://money.usnews.com/money/blogs/outside-voices-careers/articles/2016-01-12/4-traits-that-hiring-managers-want-in-a-new-employee.

Tough, P. (2016, June). How Kids Learn Resilience, *The Atlantic*. Available at http://www.theatlantic.com/magazine/toc/2016/06/.

U.S. Department of Education. (2016). Career and Technical Student Organizations. Office of Career, Technical and Adult Education. Last modified: 01/27/2016. Washington, DC: Author. Available at http://www2.ed.gov/about/offices/list/ovae/pi/cte/vso.html.

Walker, D. (2012, Nov.–Dec.). Building Robust Community Partnerships. *Techniques, 87*(8) 36-38. Available at www.acteonline.org.

chapter V

Educational Strategies to Know

Find Your "Sweet Spot"

Think back to your high school days. Do you remember thinking to yourself at least once, "Why in the heck do I have to know this stuff?" Chances are, you did. You may also remember having been assigned a chapter in a book to read or a series of problems to solve and thought to yourself that your teacher could've picked a better way to teach this.

There may be times when what some call the "drill and kill" method of teaching may be appropriate, but you have the flexibility and distinction of working in CTE. In your facility, typically, you have some open space and an area for the practice of your craft. Your innovation in that type of space should make your program exciting for your students, a place where they want to come and learn.

Competency-Based Learning

In many ways CTE has been a leader in innovational instructional strategies, and if not *the* leader, then at a minimum, the implementer of the kind of program that can take an innovation in instruction to scale. Think about "competency-based learning (CBL)," for example. Because CTE's history in curriculum development is based on a job and task analysis of an occupational specialty, the output of that analysis is information in discreet pieces, which can be categorized by "standard" (bigger category) and "competency" (sub-part of a standard). These specific terms may not be universal, but the output is still the same, and makes your curriculum transparent and intentional (The Competency-Based Education Network, 2016). This term relates to, but is not the same as the competency-based learning discussion that dominates education reform discussions (particularly in higher education) right now

Those discreet pieces of skill and knowledge build upon one another, and students have to systematically learn how the pieces fit together before the students can be considered competent in a particular area. An example may help here. In construction, building a wall involves competencies like blueprint reading, using hand and power tools, laying out structural members, laying out openings, assuring the wall is square, and sheathing the wall, among others. Once students have mastered and demonstrated these skills, they can be considered competent at building a wall.

These individual competencies can be charted and, unlike a student reading a chapter, taking a test, and receiving a grade on what they retained, CBL assures that a student has the skill and knowledge to perform. A letter grade can be based on a subjective score, but a competency is more objective. Students can perform or they can't, and if they can't, they continue to work on that competency until they *can* perform. Also, these competencies are not exclusive to one skill. Using power tools, for example, is a competency that will be used when sheathing a roof or framing a stairwell. This repetition of competencies in different environments serves to reinforce the learning along the way.

At its core, CBL is incremental, meaning that students aren't focused on an end-of-program test, but on understanding the component parts first (Heiser, 2016). It's important to use the numerous resources on competency-based learning, but good advice to the new CTE teacher would be to make sure to start from a job and task analysis, and to implement CBL into your curriculum in small doses.

Individualized Instruction

Like competency-based instruction, individualized instruction is based on discreet blocks of content that build from simple to complex (Jobs for the Future & the Council of Chief State School Officers, 2015). The idea here is that members of your class have the ability to move through your content not only at their own pace, but also, in some cases, based on their own interest level. In other words, a student may want to focus on some more advanced phase of technical content earlier than the teacher-designed schedule indicates. This does not mean that the teacher loses control of the learning, because certain units in all technical areas are basics: sanitation, measurement, safety, standard operating procedures, etc. It does mean that students can experience a bit of freedom by pursuing what they are passionate about, which research says is a definite educational motivation strategy (Jobs for the Future & the Council of Chief State School Officers, 2015, p 25).

This all sounds like a great concept, but how is it implemented, how is it tracked, and how can it assure that all students are gaining all the competencies required? As with many learning approaches, there are multiple implementation ideas. The best advice is to do a little online research and talk to your peers and supervisors about this whole topic. You will find some resources at the end of this chapter.

Here is a list of methodologies and terms you may hear associated with CTE and individualized instruction, with just enough information for you to decide whether or not you would like to continue to research each as a possibility in your classroom:

Learning packets/modules: CTE teachers understand analysis and taxonomy. Generally, CTE teachers are pretty good at breaking down the

component parts of their craft into discreet parts. As you are designing a lesson plan, try to think about ways to make this a lesson that the teacher doesn't deliver directly. Maybe students can learn from some sort of media clip (individually or in small groups); maybe they can read a technical manual segment; maybe they can learn in a group. Whatever methodology you choose, it's important to include some objective measure at the completion of the module, remembering that the assessment type should fit the instructional method (Jobs for the Future & the Council of Chief State School Officers, 2015, p 16). Commitment to this kind of instruction takes time, as the modules have to be developed and made available to students, so you may want to set a target of having six to ten modules completed each year.

Blended Learning: This usually refers to incorporating some form of online instruction and blending it with face-to-face instruction (Huguet, 2016). Typically, the online instruction is driven by a source outside the teacher's classroom, such as an online textbook or other web-based resources. The idea, though, is that the students and teacher have some flexibility. Like other forms of individualized learning, the teacher can work with students having difficulty with the material, and let others move through at their own pace. The decision to use this kind of technique is based on determining

how best to serve your students within the confines of the available resources (technology availability, online curriculum resources, open online resource guidelines, teacher's comfort level, etc.)

Cooperative Learning: Multiple scholarly articles have been written about this, as is true for many of these topics. Cooperative learning is an

educational approach in which the teacher organizes students into groups to work through tasks (Stahl, 1994) that will lead to their acquisition of technical competencies. An example may be helpful. A group of students could diagnose and troubleshoot difficulties with a boiler or heat pump. This would involve group analytical skills and cooperation, much the same as you might find on the job.

Online Asynchronous Learning: In one sense, this approach is similar to the blended learning approach mentioned above. Students work in an online environment, but they do not necessarily have to be working during their school day or on a topic that is being focused on by the rest of the class (Watson, Murin, Vashaw, Gemin, & Rapp, 2013), so they are more in control of their own learning. If students become motivated by a class discussion of gasoline engine operation to do some personal research on a more advanced unit of study, like alternative fuel and/or power sources, they should be encouraged to do so. Utilizing this approach assumes that your students have equal access to technology-based resources and it also involves the teacher monitoring the students and having policies about when these resources can be accessed.

Project-Based Learning

Project-based learning, often referred to as PBL, is an approach to learning that truly complements CTE goals. When you ask students at the end of their formal school journey, "Describe a time when you were really engaged in your learning" or "When did you feel most challenged?", inevitably the assignments or experiences they describe parallel the principles and components of a PBL assignment. CTE teachers can tap into authentic problems couched in workplace dynamics as a way to invite students to think critically. For CTE teachers who want to challenge and engage their students, PBL principles and practices can become a guide for designing classroom/lab assignments and assessments.

The Buck Institute for Education (BIE), http://www.bie.org, provides leadership and resources and creates and gathers PBL practices to assist teachers and schools. Their answer to the value of PBL includes these benefits: It makes school more engaging for students, helps address standards, and connects students and schools with the community and the real world. CTE can also provide those answers. Now, consider some ways to promote PBL in CTE settings.

Projects are a common way for CTE students to practice and showcase their technical skills. For example, marketing students create bro-chures for their CTE center for an 8th-grade tour day; culinary students host a dinner for the local school board; agriculture students rework an older-model tractor for a community member to show at the local fair; health career students set up and operate a blood pressure screening at a nearby community mall. All of these projects/experiences add value to students' learning—not only through use of technical skillsets, but also by working through multiple-step processes and interacting with others to complete the tasks. So, how do these efforts relate to project-based learning? The examples all suggest students having an authentic audience—which is a valuable PBL practice.

Another aspect of a PBL approach to consider is building opportunities into project work for students to have "voice and choice," as PBL advocates from Edutopia (http://www.edutopia.org) like to encourage. Voice and choice is a powerful way to support student engagement and investment. Imagine what it feels like (or perhaps you know) when you are working on a project and everything is dictated about how to approach the problem, what you can use to solve the problem, and what the outcome should look like. For example, how often do teachers tell students that they must share the results of their work with others in a certain way, such as a digital presentation? If we leave that decision up to students and their teammates, we are often delighted by their choices—creating a movie, setting up a blog, or modeling a technique through a demonstration.

When educators are willing to set up a project whereby students can have both a choice in how to approach the problem and a voice in the decisions that affect the project outcomes, the results are more meaningful to those students. The trick is knowing just how much up-front guidance is enough to help set a direction without diminishing student ownership of the project.

Another powerful way to leverage project learning is to provide opportunities for students to make a difference, contribute toward solving a problem, and address real issues. Just as health career students can provide blood pressure screenings, so too can they engage in deep inquiry and research into what the critical health issues are in the community and develop responsive training/interventions/assistance to share with community members.

Keep in mind that students don't need to have all the requisite skills mastered before they engage in solving a problem—PBL experiences can help create interest, a need-to-know for students that will provide reasons to want to learn the skills and concepts that propel them deeper into the project work. So, even though culinary students, for example, may not have all the skills and understandings mastered at the beginning of an investigation, such as how a school community can serve more locally-produced whole foods, the power of ownership through making a difference creates momentum and enhances the students' learning process with hands-on projects like preparing a meal for the school board

Integrated Academics

What if, as a CTE educator, you could incorporate science, technology, engineering, math (STEM) and other academic areas into your program study? Wouldn't that be incredible for many reasons?

Research provides several reasons for developing and teaching integrated lessons (Ennis & Showerman, 2011):

1. Saving class time by overlapping academic and CTE content and skills.
2. Increasing the opportunity for students to view complex issues from a broader perspective.
3. Stimulating higher levels of integrated thinking by students.
4. Decreasing curriculum fragmentation.
5. Assisting students with the increased graduation requirements implemented by many states.
6. Creating a more highly educated workforce, which should contribute to a healthier economy.

Combining CTE and academic content provides a critical connection for students to understand the relevance of scientific theories as well as literature, arts, and social sciences. How can CTE educators plan for integration? Among the many approaches to integration two that are popular include those that look at integrated curriculum and interdisciplinary curriculum. There are multiple definitions of these approaches and different labels oftentimes are applied in using them.

Probably the easiest integration implementation method is to use an integrated lesson method. A teacher reviews his or her CTE program of study and reinforces whatever content and skills match national and/or state academic standards. A middle school example of this comes from Virginia. There, math teachers teach a geometry standard to use visualization, spatial reasoning, and geometric modeling to solve problems while using the correct terms and principles. This learning is integrated with the 8th-grade technology education course and applied as students complete a balsa wood bridge building activity. Although the integrated curriculum method can begin initially with a teacher working alone, the greatest success for integration can come when the CTE teacher communicates and works closely with other teachers (in this example, math teachers).

This leads to the second method of integration that can be called an integrated unit or module, essentially a content that takes longer than one lesson to cover. Integrated units require additional time for coordination between CTE teachers and academic teachers. An example of this is the following:

1. A family and consumer sciences teacher (or life science teacher or biology teacher) explains that food sources were once living organisms made of complex molecules (carbohydrates, fats and proteins); he or she also teaches about cellular composition, single-celled and multi-celled organisms, their ecosystems, etc.

2. The culinary arts teacher discusses how these factors affect taste as well as how the human body reacts to them, incorporates how microbes affect sanitation procedures, and so on. Students gain connections between real-world actions and hopefully the information is less abstract and better retained.

In both situations, the most effective teachers will know the courses in which their students are enrolled and what overlaps of content and skills are possible (Moye, 2011).

How can you begin to create an integrated lesson plan? Well, it may initially seem overwhelming, but the following advice will help you to succeed. Select a topic or concept that seems challenging to your students. Ask them what they know about it before you teach it. Ask them if they have ever been taught something about it before, and, if so, when and where. Follow up by looking at the targeted academic curriculum and your CTE course curriculum, scanning for content or skill overlaps, and speaking to the academic teachers who teach that information. Ask them about the concept/skills related to the one that you have targeted, how they teach it, and when they teach it (if you didn't gain this information directly from your students or if you just want to confirm what they said).

Sometimes professional development focused on integration for both CTE and academic teachers can be helpful and needed. Providing in-service opportunities for teachers to come together and share information and to plan integrated lessons and skills is valuable. Experienced educators and school administrators can also provide tips and support in assisting teachers to create integrated lessons or units. The goal should be not only to plan for integration for one lesson, but also to create a long-range plan for integrated lessons/units when and wherever possible.

Remember that after each integrated lesson/unit is taught or project is completed, the CTE teacher needs to reflect on what changed for the better with his or her integrated approach, what aspects worked effectively, and what changes or improvements need to be made to improve the integrated lesson or unit for students.

Integration of CTE programs with academics enables students to better understand why academic knowledge is necessary to their CTE program, to reinforce content and training, to apply it to real-world situations, and to develop employability skills. Integration also helps them to transition from high school to work or post-secondary training through linkages with business/industry, community colleges, and universities (Blackboard Schoolwires, 2016). Not only is integration a good idea, but it is also a requirement if a school division uses federal Perkins Act funds (ACTE, 2006).

Student-Centered Learning

Think about a time when you were so caught up in a challenge, project, or task that you lost track of time. That feeling of being swept up in learning new skills both fuels students' imaginations and creates excitement for learning at the same time! Teachers are always looking for opportunities to craft learning experiences that offer students just that! Think about what opportunities encourage students to "step up". What do students really like about their learning experiences?

Students certainly like choice in assignments. They like to be challenged, but not so much that they feel they can't accomplish the goal. Students appreciate responsibility—real leadership and ownership of assignment goals and tasks. They also benefit from relevancy in what teachers ask of them—not only a personal connection to the assignment, but also a connection to real-world application of that assignment.

Generally speaking, student-centered learning requires teachers to shift their roles to facilitators of learning, versus providing all the answers and directing all the processes in the classroom (Andrade, Huff, & Brooke, 2012). A popular approach, it can take many forms in classrooms around the country. As this book is designed for CTE educators, the focus here will be on a program entitled the "Simulated Workplace," which works especially well in CTE. The West Virginia Office of Career Technical Education (2016) and its stakeholder community has created the "Simulated Workplace" as a mechanism to shift teaching and learning to a student-centered approach through student led learning. CTE programs adopt a set of protocols that support a work environment in which students take ownership for their learning.

Students take on authentic roles, crafted after industry positions such as service managers for automotive programs or head nurses for health career programs. When students are empowered to fulfill the responsibilities of a service manager or head nurse, the level of commitment and learning increases. In industry, time is money. Through a Simulated Workplace environment, students can manage projects, set productivity goals, determine what improvements are necessary to be more efficient, and reflect on how their contributions support or detract from their company's bottom line

What does this student-centered approach in CTE look like? Let's visualize students in a Simulated Workplace and some opportunities for ownership. Examples include:

- A student safety manager holds a 5-minute safety update each day to review critical equipment maintenance, review personal protective equipment (PPE), or critique an equipment shutdown procedure.
- Company employees (students) research and prepare a script for creating a video on how to properly mix mortar as a reference resource in a masonry company.
- A team reviews a section of their company handbook for possible revisions after there is a violation with tool usage.
- A student project manager facilitates a brainstorming session on the beginnings of a community effort, trying to understand

the parameters, and what skills and understandings students already bring to the tasks.

- A quality assurance manager (a student, of course!) holds a meeting to debrief on 5S organization (a term from lean manufacturing that denotes a system to improve workplace productivity through maintaining order and creating an action plan to remedy infractions).
- Students create a data wall for their company, including their company performance data on technical pre-assessments, and set goals and benchmarks. Students monitor progress and help support each other to gain more skills and earn certifications/ credentials.

Designing assignments and program goals that invite students to make decisions and take on more responsibility creates value. In order for student-centered experiences to work, teachers (or company owners in Simulated Workplace), need to be willing to "let go" of the beliefs that students cannot take on more responsibility until they have all the prerequisite skills or cannot learn unless directed by their teacher. Sarah Field (2016), Curriculum and Program Manager of Buck Institute for Education (BIE), suggests that, as teachers grow into facilitator roles, they get better at designing the supports students need and concurrently figure out when additional supports will help versus hinder.

Tools For Your Toolbox
Our first entry comes from a math teacher in West Virginia who had the opportunity to work with her CTE counterparts early in her career.

As a mathematics teacher searching for ways to inspire more students, it felt like I had won the lottery when I had an opportunity to work in a career-technical center. I quickly learned how the understandings and skills I was helping students to learn were complementary tools for students studying in various career fields. During my first week of work as an integrated math teacher, I was struck when observing several students who I knew were quiet, reserved, and compliant in their math class, just come alive in their building trades or machine tool classes—managing projects confidently, using written resources, collaborating to solve prob-lems., Seeing them so involved in their learning was a professional "aha" moment that continues to drive my philosophy to this day.

I became an investigator and interviewed CTE teachers and their students about how they applied mathematics in their field. For example, using the focus on linear equations, I learned that business students use formulas to calculate gross profit and overhead; builders must use the concept of volume to figure out how much concrete mix to use; students studying electricity embrace the classic formula of Ohm's Law constantly; and health career students use linear relationships when diluting solutions.

CTE teachers provide the magical context so important for deeper acquisition of mathematics, science, and literacy understandings. Being willing to collaborate with academic colleagues on identifying connections, sharing how each teacher approaches concepts and the terminology they use, and co-creating challenging questions/problems that reflect authentic situations and meet a variety of academic standards, is key.

A culinary teacher once shared with me that he was astounded when he finally figured out why his students were having trouble following his work on recipe conversions. He had a large group of Culinary I students from several different source schools. He hit on a gold mine of insight when he asked a question by accident.

"Ryan, how is it that you write/show division of two numbers at your school?"

Ryan showed him the symbols and the process he understood from his math classes in middle school.

Immediately, other students disagreed, and said, "That's not how we learned it!"

The class figured out there were at least four different ways that students understood division—so when their culinary teacher used an unfamiliar method, it was like listening to someone speak a foreign language.

Students benefit when their teachers appreciate each other's worlds and explore CT-academic connections.

Our second *Tool,* which comes from a machining teacher in West Virginia, discusses the concept of student-centered learning in the "Simulated Workplace."

Imagine, instead of walking into a classroom full of students that are disconnected and bored, that you walk into a "company" with "employees" that are engaged and eager to learn. Welcome to Precision Machining Company (PMC), a Simulated Workplace.

In PMC my teaching style has changed from a traditional teacher to a coach and mentor. I no longer just stand around lecturing and telling my students what to do, but I am a Company Owner, assisting employees through the learning process. I no longer just answer questions, but I challenge my students to find the answers. My responsibility is to make PMC as close to real world as possible. With that in mind, employees are required to punch in and out every day. If they are not going to be at work, they are required to call in. Employees will be randomly drug tested. Employees will work independently as well as on teams. Good communication skills are a must.

Employees of PMC are responsible for scheduling and planning the steps necessary to complete the tasks at hand. At the beginning of each six-week period, employees are given a packet containing all of the requirements for that six-week period. It is up to the employee to create a plan of how he or she will complete the tasks. In addition to a personal plan, employees will hold positions in the company. They may be the Production Manager, Shop Foreman, Safety Manager, or Tool Room Manager, just to name a few. These positions will rotate, giving each employee the opportunity to experience what it is like to be in charge of a team.

The typical day at PMC goes something like this: We start with a three-to- five minute employee-led safety meeting. The Production Manager will hold a production meeting to plan the day's work. The Shop Foreman will ensure that the work is completed. Employees will record progress on the production board. Any issues that arise must follow the chain of command. If the management team cannot resolve an issue, it will be brought to the Company Owner.

Each Simulated Workplace is governed by 12 protocols. These protocols will help to ensure that we maintain high-performance Simulated Workplaces. The protocols are: Student-Led Companies; Application/Interview Structure; Formal Attendance System; Drug Free Work Zones; 5S Environment; Safe Work Areas; Workplace Teams; Project-Based Learning/Student Engagement; Company Name and Handbook; Company Meetings; Onsite Business Reviews; and Accountability—data review, reporting, and technical assessments.

I enjoy coming to work every day to see what the employees of PMC will come up with next. I do not have to imagine a place where employees are eager and engaged, as I get to be a part of it every day. For more information, visit www.simulatedworkplace.com.

Our last entry includes two examples of curriculum-mapping activities that help connect technical areas with math concepts. These examples were taken from some work done by the National Research Center on connecting regular education with CTE. This curriculum mapping is a first step when integrating content, and we thought the examples might provide a good start.

CURRICULUM MAPPING CTE PROGRAM—Health Occupations

CTE UNIT/TOPIC	CTE CONCEPTS	MATH CONCEPTS
Human Structure and Function	Compare cell, tissue, organ, and body systems relationships	Solving linear equations; reading and interpreting graphs and charts; problem solving involving statistical data; ratio and proportion
Health Care and Delivery System	Vital signs; height and weight charts; intake and output; percent of burns; body planes; range of motion	Solving linear equations; reading and interpreting graphs and charts; problem solving involving statistical data; ratio and proportion

CURRICULUM MAPPING CTE PROGRAM—Automotive

CTE UNIT/TOPIC	CTE CONCEPTS	MATH CONCEPTS
Engine Performance	On-Board Diagnostic and Scan Tools	Whole numbers; binary math basics; charts and graphs; reading and writing percentages; comparing numbers; angles; degrees of rotation; temperature measurement; ratios
Brakes	Braking Components	Metric to English conversions; whole numbers; comparing numbers; temperature; decimals; inequalities; positive and negative numbers; linear measurement; micrometers

KEY LEARNINGS:

1. Make learning matter for your students.
2. Competencies build toward skill.
3. Competency-based learning is incremental.
4. Individual learning packets or plans enable students to move ahead quickly.
5. Add variety to your instructional delivery.
6. Consider incorporating project-based learning.
7. Teaching an integrated lesson plan reinforces regular education concepts and technical competence.
8. The Simulated Workplace is a means to motivate students.

RELATED CONTENT THAT MAY BE OF INTEREST:

Andrade, G., Huff, K. & Brooke, G. (2012). Assessment in the Context of Student-centered Learning: The Students at the Center Series. Boston, MA: Jobs for the Future. Available at http://www.jff.org/sites/default/files/publications/materials/Assessing%20LearningPDF.pdf.

Blackboard Schoolwires. (2002-2016). Integrated Academics. Blackboard, Inc. Available at www.vbisd.org/Page/547.

Association for Career and Technical Education. (2006). Perkins Act of 2006: The Official Guide. Alexandria, VA

Buck Institute for Education (BIE). (2016). Why Project Based Learning (PBL)? Available at http://www.bie.org.

Competency-Based Education Network. (2016). What is Competency-Based Education? Available at http://www.cbenetwork.org/.

Edutopia. (2016). Resources. Available at http://www.edutopia.org/.

Ennis, M., & Showerman, R. (2011). Online resources to support academic & CTE integration. Presented at Michigan Career Conference. Available at www.michigancareerconference.org.

Field, S, (2016, June 3). Scaffolding Content and Process in PBL. Buck Institute for Education. Available at http://www.bie.org/blog/scaffolding_content_and_process_in_pbl.

Heiser, E.A. (2016, September). CBE in CTE: The Perfect Fit. Techniques. 91(6), 14-18. Available at www.acteonline.org.

Huguet, M. C. (2016, April). A Blended Approach. Techniques. 91(4), 28-32. Available at www.acteonline.org.

Jobs for the Future & the Council of Chief State School Officers. (2015, August). Educator Competencies for Personalized, Learner-Centered Teaching. Boston, MA: Jobs for the Future. Available at http://files.eric.ed.gov/fulltext/ED560785.pdf.

Moye, J. (2011, March). Real integration—where the rubber meets the road. Techniques, 86(3), 48-51. Available at www.acteonline.org.

Stahl, R.J. (1994, March). The Essential Elements of Cooperative Learning in the Classroom. ERIC Digest. ED370881. Available at http://www.ericdigests.org/1995-1/elements.htm.

Watson, J., Murin, A., Vashaw, L., Gemin, B., & Rapp, C. (2013). Keeping Pace with K-12 Online & Blended Learning: An Annual Review of Policy and Practice, 2013. Grand Rapids, MI: Evergreen Education Group. Available at http://files.eric.ed.gov/fulltext/ED565714.pdf.

West Virginia Office of Career Technical Education. (2016). Simulated Workplace. Charleston, WV: WV Department of Education (WVDE). Available at http://wvde.state.wv.us/simulated-workplace/.

chapter VI

Using Evaluation Results for Growth

Feedback Please!

Try to think about a profession with no real standards, where there's nothing to be measured against to know if you're doing a good job. Maybe something in entertainment, like stand-up comedians. Now, you could probably argue that the number of laughs they get or the amount of interaction with their audiences is a standard of measurement, at least a pass/fail one.

Generally speaking, every occupation has a standard to which workers are held. In fact, for areas in which public safety or sanitation are a concern, many states require a certification or a license to practice that occupation. Shaping young minds is no different and, given that education is by law a state responsibility (U.S. Department of Education, 2016), your state has a process that requires you to maintain that license. That process involves an individual evaluation of your performance. This evaluation is required in most states. As a professional CTE teacher, it's important that you use this evaluation to your advantage as one of your tools for measuring your own personal growth.

Most of these evaluations are required an- 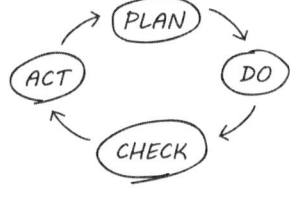 nually, so multiple times each year, so you'll have a roadmap for improvement from year to year, as well as one that uses data over the course of your career (longitudinally). This chapter looks at a variety of levels of evaluation and provides some background on each of them.

Why Evaluation is Important

Evaluation in education can be viewed from a variety of perspectives, an important one being from a national level, which has been driven by  federal legislation such as the Elementary and Secondary Education Act (ESEA) of 1965 and subsequent reauthorizations; including No Child Left Behind (NCLB) in 2001, the 2009 Race to the Top program Act (RTTT), and Every Student Succeeds Act of 2015 (ESSA). These laws have all been focused on equal access, high standards, and accountability. The Individuals with Disabilities Education Act (IDEA) of 1975 established education rights for individuals with disabilities, and the current authorization of the Carl D. Perkins Career and Technical Education Act establishes performance measures and standards for CTE programs and student achievement. Evaluation and accountability are important components of all current federal education legislation, and they all link federal funding to accountability. To some degree, this measure is needed to assess the return on the investment of federal tax dollars, but at their hearts, these measures were designed to encourage instructional quality and continuous improvement.

The Constitution of the United States defines education as a state's right, meaning that each state has the right to determine the laws governing public education. States that accept federal money (and they all do) are subject to the accountability measures and standards established by federal legislation. Under both the ESEA and Carl D. Perkins legislation, each state is required to prepare a plan that addresses how they will achieve the performance standards required under the federal act and define how performance will be evaluated. Typically, a state's plan addresses progress measured over a period of years (see Pennsylvania Dept. of Education, 2014a); failing to achieve the standards identified in the state plan can potentially result in the loss of federal funding for that state.

At the federal level, evaluation can be focused on school, CTE program, teacher performance, and student achievement. Regardless of the method of assessment used in a state, each state has developed baseline data and reasonable objectives for gains in federal performance standards. Just as the federal program can penalize states for an inability to meet their goals, states can also withhold funding for CTE programs based on the state's plan and benchmark criteria in the state's evaluation and accountability system.

As a CTE teacher, you should have a basic knowledge of the federal and state legislation that affects your school, program, students, and you as a professional educator. Chapter I provided a concise summary of the important elements of various federal legislation beginning with the Smith-Hughes Act of 1917; if you study the evolution of the legislation, you quickly see accountability rising in prominence. As mentioned, part of the reason is accounting for spending U.S. tax dollars, but the other reason is program improvement.

Funding Makes a Difference

The governor in each state prepares an annual state budget in which education is almost always the greatest expenditure. As a result, governors, state legislators, and taxpayers are demanding higher levels of account-

ability than ever before. Parents expect their students to be prepared for success in post-secondary education and in their chosen careers. This means that state-funded secondary programs have to provide a consistently strong foundation.

States are accountable for the implementation of federal and state laws and regulations. The method of delivering CTE can vary from state to state, just as the method of evaluating the success of CTE in each state may differ. Some states maintain strong control over public education, requiring compliance to a core state academic and CTE curriculum, program of study or task list, and a state end-of-program assessment. Other states allow more local control of education, and local school boards or counties determine graduation requirements, curriculum, and CTE delivery methods.

Because states are responsible for the implementation of federal and state laws and regulations, they do provide state requirements for compliance to federal legislation like the performance measures of the Carl D. Perkins Act. In addition, state evaluation plans must comply with other federal law, including Title VI and Title VII of the Civil Rights Act of 1964; Title IX of the Education Amendments of 1972; Section 504 of the Rehabilitation Act of 1973; the Age Discrimination in Employment Act of 1967; and the Americans with Disabilities Act of 1990 (Pennsylvania Department of Education, 2014b).

In support of the accountability indicators under the Perkins Act, some states require an end-of-program assessment for students who complete a CTE program; states increasingly rely on services like NOCTI for end-of-program assessments, credentialing, and the data required for CTE program improvements predicated upon student achievement. Quality third-party assessments provide performance data and comparisons to baseline competency data at a variety of levels (national, state, and local).

State evaluations and compliance reviews can result in a CTE program being closed. Funding can also be withheld from the state, along with Perkins funds, for a period of time, until the CTE program achieves the standards and meets requirements as determined by the state. The evaluation can be in the form of an individual or team from the state department of education or public instruction performing an on-site evaluation of the school and/or program. A state evaluation may also be conducted by analyzing performance data submitted to the state by the school. Any form of evaluation performed by the state can result in the loss of state approval and funding. It can also impact a school or program's state grant eligibility.

Federal, State, and School Board Priorities

Most career technical schools and colleges seek a third-party accreditation and/or external evaluation of the organization and its preparation to meet and/or exceed federal, state, and local goals and priorities. Schools typically prepare a strategic plan and adopt policies and standard practices that facilitate the implementation and attainment of mandatory and adopted goals and priorities.

A third-party assessment or accreditation review usually follows a self-study of the organization's preparedness for the external evaluation. It may be conducted by a number of different agencies such as a state team of education and business professionals, a regional commission, and/or a professional association. In some instances, external audits are performed on federal grants such as the use of Perkins funds and by state agencies for the purpose of determining compliance to state regulations and standards.

Without going into extensive detail here, there are other entities that perform periodic programmatic evaluations of schools as a whole. One example can be found in the regional commissions like the Middle States Commission on Elementary and Secondary Schools (www.msa-cess.org), for which schools complete a self-study for the purpose of growth and improvement. Middle States has twelve standards specifically for career-technical schools (Middle States Association of Colleges and Schools, 2012); once accredited, the accreditation period is seven years. The Council on Occupational Education or COE (www.council.org) provides accreditation services to post-secondary occupational education institutions and requires an annual renewal of accreditation. The COE standards are summarized in their self-study manual (2016).

Lastly, an arm of the Southern Regional School Board (SREB), the High Schools That Work program (HSTW; see www.sreb.org/about-hstw) emphasizes high expectations and rigorous academics for all students, including CTE students. Member schools implement 10 Key Practices and Goals for changing student expectations, what they're taught, and how (SREB, 2016). HSTW is the largest comprehensive school reform program for high schools in the U.S. (Young, Cline, King, Jackson, & Timberlake, 2011). The program is based on the belief that most students can master complex academic and technical concepts if schools create an environment that encourages students to make the effort to succeed. HSTW/SREB staff can conduct a desktop audit of a school and produce a case study with useful information.

Program Evaluation

Some states allow local school boards or operating boards to establish CTE programs and teach content and skills as guided by various local occupational advisory committees. Other states provide CTE program development criteria and strict compliance for the continued state approval of CTE programs. Typically, states that provide supplemental funding or subsidy dollars do require adherence to specific criteria for the award and use of state funding. On-site compliance reviews are a common accountability measure for this kind of evaluation. All of the compliance reviews studied for this chapter required some form of teacher evaluation, or at least a description of how they are used as part of the process.

Credentialing Evaluation

In order to provide students with business and industry credentials, CTE schools and individual programs sometimes apply to trade associations, or national or state organizations for accreditation. Accreditation allows the school and program to conduct specific occupational assessments and award various certifications and credentials or may function as a quality "seal of approval. The process usually involves a self-study comparing the school and, primarily, the program to specific industry criteria. The criteria range from teacher qualifications and staff possession of mastery-level industry credentials, lab size and configuration, equipment and tools lists, and various other criteria including industry advisory committee support.

Each industry-accrediting agency publishes its own criteria, but all accrediting agencies generally perform an on-site assessment after an analysis of the self-study submission. Upon completion of the self-study and on-site evaluation, the accrediting agency will notify the school and program of its status with regard to approval or additional preparation required prior to approval. This type of accreditation can be considered a standard of excellence for the school and CTE program, as well as an emblem of quality for CTE students and graduates.

Teacher Evaluation: Making it Personal

Teacher evaluation serves several purposes. It satisfies a statutory requirement and provides a legal basis for determining continued employment or termination of a professional employee. More importantly, teacher evaluation provides a vehicle for continued improvement and relevant professional development.

Teacher evaluation provides a system for accountability to professional standards, practices, and ethics. An example of one system is the popular Danielson framework (Danielson, 2008). It provides an indicator of teacher performance as measured against federal, state, and local standards and expectations. This chapter is not intended to provide a comprehensive analysis of teacher evaluations. It does, however, emphasize the importance of accountability with regard to your role as a CTE teacher in support of federal, state, and school requirements.

Your first level of accountability in CTE is to the student and his/her success. Fortunately, the indicators in federal and state legislation address the same issues that are important to students, their parents, and employers. You are a professional educator directly responsible for your students' achievement in CTE. Being held accountable for that achievement is a professional expectation.

Another important level of account-ability is to the employer. Competition in the global economy has driven the demand for a technically-skilled work-

force (Sussman, 2016), and CTE is the primary supplier of technical workers. Secondary and post-secondary CTE programs play a vital role in shaping the competiveness of America's workforce. The demand for higher skills and knowledge from employers increases the demand on both schools and students to achieve higher levels of academic and technical knowledge. Employer evaluations of cooperative education students and feedback on recent graduates are a direct reflection on your professional abilities.

The last level of accountability is to yourself; as a CTE professional, you should plan time for reflection, analysis, and adjustment. This was mentioned generally in Chapter X of Foster, Foster, Hornberger, and McNally (2015) regarding the close of the school year. Taking time to reflect is touted by educational media as being one of the common threads identifying quality teachers and teaching. You can see reflection mentioned in the national CTE teacher quality standards (National Board for Professional Teaching Standards, 2014), and many CTE professionals will take time during longer breaks from teaching to reflect on their goals, their style, their delivery, others' evaluations of them, and their student outcomes. Remember, though, that reflection is only part of the process. Taking an objective look at all the information and considering patterns and hard data should always lead to adjustments that are part of a continuous personal self-improvement cycle.

What Does an Effective Evaluation Look Like?

From the authors' perspective, an effective performance evaluation is one that enhances both personal and instructional growth. With that criterion in mind, multiple factors come in to play: frequency, objectivity, purpose, and follow-up are all important considerations. Without analyzing each of these, some hints might help in determining effectiveness.

It is unquestionably difficult to take one look at something complex and evaluate it. If you were seeing an automobile for the first time, would you understand how to operate it, let alone how to make it more effective? Generally speaking, the more people observe something working, the better understanding they have of it, and the better able they are to evaluate effectiveness. But, it can be asked, effectiveness as judged by whom?

If we go back to our car analogy, effectiveness as judged by an auto technician would be different than effectiveness as judged by a driver or a driving instructor. The point here is that consideration of multiple perspectives is generally more effective than assessment based on one single observation. The purpose of the evaluation should also be asked: is it a simple pass/fail, or is it more of an evaluation against a known set of standards? Lastly, how much time is spent in following up the evaluation? This is a very important part of the process, yet is also frequently the most overlooked. A personnel evaluation in education is a snapshot in time; discussing this evaluation with the individual being evaluated can yield insight that usually provides most helpful information.

Using an Evaluation to Improve?

When you were a new CTE teacher, your supervisor probably watched you interacting with your class numerous times those first few years. Most states do formal observations at least twice a year and, in some cases, have peers provide observations as well. The audience of this book is the third-year CTE teacher who has come into the education field without the benefit of a college degree  in teaching. So by this time, you should already have had four to six formal observations from others about the effectiveness of your instruction. You may also have another set of observations from your peers. These reports about your effectiveness should be analyzed; you need to work  with your supervisor to find common themes on which to focus. Is there a recurring theme regarding safety in your lab that was noticed by multiple observers? Was there something about your questioning techniques or about your evaluation of projects or assignments? Whatever the issue, use the feedback as a way to make your instruction and your students' success rate better. The key point is that both teachers and administrators need to develop the ability to use data from multiple sources, e.g., evaluations and assessments, to nurture a culture of continuous improvement (Foster, Hodes & Pritz, 2014) and use data as a vehicle for learning, either to validate teacher efforts or to justify needed improvements (Elgart, 2016). Data should be used as a flashlight to shine a light on what's working and to inform professional growth, not as a hammer to make teachers feel like failures (Rosenberg, 2013).

Tools For Your Toolbox

The first entry in the *Tools* section for this chapter comes from a former state director in California. His narrative focuses on a program evaluation that is used for approved CTE programs. Though it is not a personnel evaluation, we identified three sections of the eleven-part evaluation that included expectations for teachers implementing successful CTE programming. The abbreviated list follows, but the entire list can be found on the California Department of Education website.

California Department of Education
Career Technical Education (CTE)
11 Elements of a High-Quality CTE Program
Self-Review Tool

Update 09/15

Yes	No		1. LEADERSHIP AT ALL LEVELS	
			What is being Assessed	Evidence
		1A.	The CTE pathways are articulated with post-secondary and industry through programs of study, formal articulation agreements, and dual enrollment.	• Dual Enrollment information • Articulation Agreements
		1B.	Local district administrators participate in CTE professional development regarding the benefits of CTE and the management of CTE within the larger context of educational improvement to serve all students.	• Dates and Names of Activities
		1C.	Investment is made to provide support for CTE leadership at the local level to ensure that CTE administrators, teacher(s), and counseling and instructional leaders have sufficient time and resources to implement system improvements and to work with their counterparts in other programs.	• Dates and Names of Activities

Yes	No		2. HIGH-QUALITY CURRICULUM AND INSTRUCTION	
			What is being Assessed	Evidence
		2A.	The CTE Model Curriculum Standards are the basis for content of courses offered. Curriculum addresses "Pathway" standards within the program pathway(s) and course sequence.	• Course Outlines • Course Catalog • Local CTE Plan • Review Curriculum Document
		2B.	Career paths have been identified and can be found on a chart or diagram in the CTE Plan.	• Local CTE Plan
		2C.	The CTE program has classroom-linked work-based learning and work experience education opportunities through strengthened industry partnerships; effective coordination with Regional Occupation Center/Programs (ROC/P); adult schools; Work Experience Education; Cooperative Work Experience Education programs; and a systematic review of policies and practices addressing barriers to access, including insurance, liability, and other issues.	• List of Work Based Learning (WBL) Sites • Percentage of Students Participating
		2D.	The school master schedule allows students to follow the recommended sequence of CTE courses to complete the selected career path(s).	• Master Schedule • Course Catalog

Yes	No		What is being Assessed	Evidence
		2E.	Students gain experience in, and an under-standing of, all aspects of industry.	• WBL Experiences • Review Curriculum Document • Lesson Plans
		2F.	Technology is incorporated into program instruction.	• Program-Based Software • Program-Related Technology and Advanced Equipment
		2G	There is collaboration between academic and CTE teachers.	• Agenda • Minutes • Sign-In Sheets
			CTE courses are industry certified, meet high school graduation requirements, University of California a-g (UC a-g) credit, or are articulated with a community college.	• Copy of Certification or Licensure • Copy of UC A-G Approval List; Articulation Agreements

9. SKILLED FACULTY AND PROFESSIONAL DEVELOPMENT

Yes	No		What is being Assessed	Evidence
		9A	Every CTE teacher has the appropriate credential(s) for teaching the subject(s) as-signed, as well as documented employment experience outside of education in the program area taught.	• Approved by Local Credential offices
		9B	Based on the previous year's records, every CTE teacher teaching at least half-time, attends a minimum of four professional development activities.	• List of Teacher Technical Development Activities Such as Staff Exchange, Technical Conferences, Industry Certification Training, Etc.
		9C.	The CTE staff meets a minimum of twice a month. (This criterion does not apply to single person departments - mark column N/A = Not Applicable.)	• Staff Meeting Minutes
		9D.	A written record of minutes of action taken during CTE staff meetings is kept in Department files.	• Staff Meeting Minutes

Our second tool is a standardized state evaluation form from the state of Pennsylvania. Essentially, it is the state's responsibility to determine satisfactory or unsatisfactory ratings for teachers within the Commonwealth. This is accomplished through completion of the form below. There are additional instructions that can be found online, but we wanted to display the categories, as we thought they might be a helpful point of focus.

Commonwealth of Pennsylvania	DEPARTMENT OF EDUCATION	333 Market St., Harrisburg, PA 17126-0333

CLASSROOM TEACHER RATING FORM

PDE 82-1 (7/14)

Last Name	First	Middle
District/LEA	School	
Rating Date	Evaluation (Check One)	☐ Periodic ☐ Semi-annual ☐ Annual

(A) Classroom Teacher Observation and Practice

Domain	Title	*Rating* (A)	Factor (B)	Earned Points (A x B)	Max Points
I.	Planning & Preparation		20%		0,60
II.	Classroom Environment		30%		0,90
III.	Instruction		30%		0,90
IV.	Professional Responsibilities		20%		0,60
(1) Classroom Teacher Observation and Practice Rating					3,00

Domain Rating Assignment 0 to 3 Point Scale (A)	
Rating	Value
Failing	0
Needs Improvement	1
Proficient	2
Distinguished	3

(B) Multiple Measures - Building Level Data, Teacher Specific Data, and Elective Data

Building Level Score (0 - 107)	
(2) Building Level Score Converted to 3 Point Rating	

(3) Teacher Specific Rating	
(4) Elective Rating	

(C) Final Classroom Teacher Effectiveness Rating - All Measures

Measure	Rating (C)	Factor (D)	Earned Points (C x D)	Max Points
(1) Observation and Practice Rating		50%		1,50
(2) Building Level Rating (or substitute)*		15%		0,45
(3) Teacher Specific Rating (or substitute)*		15%		0,45
(4) Elective Rating (or substitute)*		20%		0,60
	Total Earned Points			3,00

Conversion to Performance Rating	
Total Earned Points	Rating
0.00 - 0.49	Failing
0.50 - 1.49	Needs Improvement
1.50 - 2.49	Proficient
2.50 - 3.00	Distinguished
Performance Rating	

* Substitutions permissible pursuant to 22 Pa. Code §§ 19.1 (IV)(a)(5), (b)(2)(ix), (b)(3)(vi), (c)(3), or (d)

☐ Rating: Professional Employee,   OR   ☐ Rating: Temporary Professional Employee

I certify that the above-named employee for the period beginning _____ and ending _____ has received a performance rating of:
(month/day/year)   (month/day/year)

☐ Distinguished   ☐ Proficient   ☐ Needs Improvement   ☐ Failing

resulting in a final rating of:

☐ Satisfactory   ☐ Unsatisfactory

A performance rating of Distinguished, Proficient or Needs Improvement shall be considered satisfactory, except that the second Needs Improvement rating issued by the same employer within 10 years of the first final rating of Needs Improvement where the employee is in the same certification shall be considered unsatisfactory. A rating of Failing shall be considered unsatisfactory.

_____   _____
Date   Designated Rater / Position: Date   Chief School Administrator

I acknowledge that I have read the report and that I have been given an opportunity to discuss it with the rater. My signature does not necessarily mean that I agree with the performance evaluation.

_____
Date   Signature of Employee

Our third tool is from a teacher in Florida who discusses her first teacher observation and evaluation. We think she provides a couple of really good ideas that you can learn from too!

Understanding state evaluation systems and using them to grow is an essential part of becoming a professional educator. However, in this era of accountability, there are as many state evaluations as there are states; in addition, many schools and states are updating or completely changing their methods of teacher evaluation. But that doesn't mean you have to be in the dark. Before your evaluation, ask to go over it with your evaluator. It is important to know ahead of time what you are being evaluated on!

For example, in my first year of teaching, during my very first professional educator evaluation, I saw my principal making tally marks in columns. I couldn't help but notice that it looked like she was making a lot of tally marks! I lost some of my lesson "steam," and afterward I felt like a complete failure. When it was my scheduled time to meet with my principal and go over my evaluation, I was filled with trepidation and slunk dejectedly into her office.

"What's wrong?" she asked cheerfully. "You did great!"

"What?" I stammered, "I-I-I saw you making a lot of tally marks in columns. I figured one of the columns probably was good, and the other one was probably bad, and it was too many on each side ..." I stopped talking because she was laughing so hard.

She showed me the evaluation form. The columns were for instances of specific teaching techniques observed, and both column indicators were positive. I had aced my first observation; however, because I hadn't fully informed myself ahead of time, I had no idea what I was actually being evaluated on. Yes, a day or two before the scheduled observation, I had asked a busy veteran teacher what to expect, but she had just quickly said not to worry and just to plan a good lesson.

I followed her advice, but you should follow mine: Ask to see the evaluation criteria long before your evaluation, and review it just as you would review what is on an upcoming test with your students.

And then, follow her advice: Plan a good lesson, and don't worry.

KEY LEARNINGS:

1. Formal evaluations and observations can be the roadmaps to instructional improvement.
2. Results of evaluations show a return on investment of state tax dollars.
3. Observation and evaluation of CTE teachers vary from state to state.
4. Program evaluations can provide valuable instructional improvement information.
5. Third-party industry evaluations also provide valuable data.
6. You are accountable to the students you teach.
7. An effective evaluation is clear in purpose.
8. Analyze outside feedback for patterns and use them for instructional improvement.

RELATED CONTENT THAT MAY BE OF INTEREST:

Council On Occupational Education (COE). (2016). *The Self-Study Manual, 2016 Edition.* Atlanta, GA: Author. Available at http://www.council.org/manuals/.

Danielson, C. (2008). *The handbook for enhancing professional practice: using the framework for teaching in your school.* ASCD: Alexandria, VA.

Elgart, M.A. (2016, September). Creating state accountability systems that help schools improve. *Phi Delta Kappan,* 98(1) 26-30.

Foster, J.C., Foster, P., Hornberger, C. & McNally, K. (2015). *Your First Year in CTE: 10 More Things to Know, chapter X.* Alexandria, VA: ACTE.

Foster, J., Hodes, C.L., & Pritz, S.G. (2014). *Putting your data to work: Improving instruction in CTE.* Alexandria, VA: ACTE.

RELATED CONTENT THAT MAY BE OF INTEREST, continued:

Middle States Association of Colleges and Schools. (2012). Standards for Career and Technical Institutions. Philadelphia, PA: Author. Available at http://www.msa-cess.org/Customized/uploads/Accreditation/Standards%20for%20Accreditation-CT%20Institutions%202012.pdf.

National Board for Professional Teaching Standards. (2014). *NBPTS Career and Technical Education Standards, second edition.* Arlington, VA: Author. Available at http://boardcertifiedteachers.org/sites/default/files/EAYA-CTE.pdf.

Pennsylvania Department of Education. (2014a). *Comprehensive Planning Career and Technical Center Planning Offline Guidance Tool.* Harrisburg, PA: Author. Available at http://compplanning.wiki.caiu.org/home.

Pennsylvania Department of Education. (2014b). Educator Effectiveness Administrative Manual. Harrisburg, PA: Author. Available at http://www.education.pa.gov/Documents/Teachers-Administrators/Educator%20Effectiveness/Educator%20Effectiveness%20Administrative%20Manual.pdf.

Rosenberg, H. (2013). Embracing the use of data for continuous program improvement. *Family Involvement Network of Educators (FINE) Newsletter,* 5(3). Retrieved September 6, 2016, from http://www.hfrp.org/family-involvement/fine-family-involvement-network-of-educators/fine-newsletter-archive/september-fine-newsletter-creating-a-culture-of-continuous-improvement.

Sussman, A. L. (2016, September 1). As skill requirements increase, more manufacturing jobs go unfilled. *The Wall Street Journal.* Available at http://www.wsj.com/.

U.S. Department of Education. (2016). The Federal Role in Education. Washington, DC: Author. Available at http://www2.ed.gov/about/overview/fed/role.html.

Young, J., Cline, F., King, T., Jackson, A. & Timberlake, A. (2011, August). *High Schools That Work: Program Description, Literature Review, and Research Findings.* Princeton, NJ: Educational Testing Service.

chapter VII
The Value of Employability Skills

My Life Coach is Me!

Uh-oh! You just started a new teaching job in a new city, and now you have a molar throbbing! You search online for dentists located in your area and read about their backgrounds including educational histories and certifications/degrees, their professional associations, the awards or recognitions they have achieved, their office locations, and so forth. Generally, you are gathering information about their *technical* skills and their degrees. You are researching the schools they went to, what kind of experience they have, and what kinds of services their offices provide, such as extraction, restoration, implants, x-ray diagnostics, etc.

You finally decide on one dentist who seems to possess the skills and the background that you expect. You make an appointment and have that nasty, painful tooth fixed. Then you consider whether you will go back to that same dentist the next time you need some dental work done. How good a job did he/she do in numbing your tooth, taking x-rays, filling the tooth—most of which we consider technical skills?

Not surprisingly, you will probably make that decision based on not only how you thought and felt during the process of having your cavity taken care of, but also on how that dentist greeted you, how he or she communicated about the process, and how you were treated during that initial visit. These skills, which some refer to as soft skills, may determine whether that person will become your regular dentist or not.

Let's Talk Terminology

How are these employability skills described? They are skills that characterize relationships with other people and/or how you approach life and work. Similar terms are social skills, soft skills, transferable skills, interpersonal skills, foundational skills, and people skills. The Employment and Training Administration (2016) has several samples of what are known as competency models for each occupational pathway. In those models, the categories given are personal effectiveness competencies (initiative, integrity, etc.) and workplace competencies (planning, teamwork, resource utilization, etc.).

The competency models contain some non-technical competencies recognized as necessary across all occupations, such as planning, working with other people on a project, and communicating with supervisors, co-workers, and clients. Those skills are the personal character traits or qualities that people possess and that make them who they are: their attitudes, habits, and interactions with others. Such skills assist in the (hopefully effective and efficient) completion of tasks and projects, whether at work, at home, or at play. Employing these skills, along with technical skills and knowledge, improves how people interact with colleagues and customers; they influence how people feel about their jobs and how others perceive them (McKay, Nov. 24, 2015).

How do these soft skills differ from technical skills? Technical skills include skills and knowledge needed to complete a job. Examples for carpentry skills could include estimating a project, laying out rafters, or raising a wall. Examples for childcare skills might include planning lessons in a unit, creating activities for the kids, or understanding human development. Technical skills are necessary in order to operate in a particular workplace. These skills can be taught and, once taught, the resulting competencies can be verified through performance testing.

Today's employers want employees who can demonstrate their technical skills, but who possess important employability skills as well. Employability skills are important to help any organization increase its productivity, create greater harmony among workers and clients, and strive for company success and longevity. Some employability skills are learned as people grow up with family and friends, but other skills need to be purposefully practiced on a regular basis before and during employment.

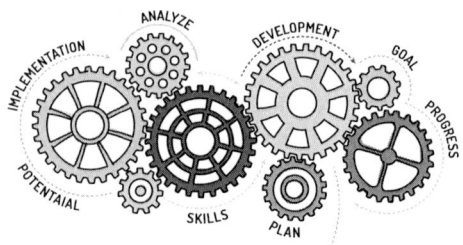

Productivity

Importance of Employability Skills to Business/Industry

Some say that employability skills may be just as important as technical skills in determining the levels of success for an individual in the workplace (Neves, 2016). However, soft skills can be some of the hardest skills to learn and develop for some people. It can also be difficult to quantify their impact on an individual's success. But, fortunately, soft skills can be learned and developed; that's a good thing because, to get and keep a job, you need a repertoire of both technical and non-technical skills!

Three major business surveys (Partnership for 21st Century Skills, 2008; National Association of Colleges and Employers [NACE], 2009; and American Management Association [AMA], 2010) identified the top-rated skills important for 21st century employees. The survey results were as follows (Hodge, 2011):

21st Century Survey	NACE	AMA
Oral Communications	Communications	Communications
Teamwork	Teamwork	Collaboration/Teamwork
Ethics/Social Responsibility	Analytical	Critical Thinking/Problem Solving
Professionalism	Technical	Creativity/Innovation
Reading Comprehension	Strong Work Ethic	

Note that most of these skills fall into the category of soft skills.

An article entitled, "Why Soft Skills Matter," (MindTools, 1996-2016) stated that if your organization is good at getting clients but not so good at keeping them, chances are that you have a soft skills gap. If you have high staff turnover and need to keep retraining employees, or if you have lots of managers but no real leaders, those are considered soft skills gaps too. Although technical skills may get an applicant's foot in the first door, people skills are what open most of the other doors to come.

Among those soft skills crucial for career success are work ethic, attitude, communication skills, emotional intelligence, ability to see "the big picture," and resource management. A typical workplace is very dynamic and requires good communication skills such as listening, presenting ideas, encouraging an open and supportive network for people to express themselves and their ideas, collaborating, coaching and mentoring others, resolving conflicts as they occur, and building and maintaining personal and professional relationships, among others. The better these skills are developed, the more likely the success of establishing long-term employees, colleagues, supervisors, clients, and other stakeholders within that workplace.

Getting the Message to Students

The Skills You Need Newsletter (2011-2016) provides an article on seven of the most important soft skills:

1. **Communication Skills:** Used in building relationships and rapport leading to long-term relationships; listening well and varying communication to suit the circumstances.
2. **Making Decisions:** Being able to choose the best option; valued by employers.
3. **Self-Motivation:** Being able to take personal initiative for both initiating and accomplishing projects, without the need for constant supervision or direction.
4. **Leadership Skills:** Usually those skills that we least expect someone to develop on their own, but can be developed further, often through leadership training and/or leadership courses.
5. **Team-Working Skills:** Good communication skills, particularly good listening skills, help to build rapport and improve teamwork.
6. **Creativity and Problem Solving Skills:** Highly valued because they are hard to develop; some people seem to have these abilities more than others, but creativity and problem solving skills can be developed.
7. **Time Management (and ability to work under pressure):** Some people believe that these two skills are more an attitude than skills, but they also can be developed and honed; they are highly valued by employers, useful for organizing a family or a team, and for making sure that the job gets done.

The federal Office of Career Technical and Adult Education (OCTAE) has an "Employability Skills Framework" (http://cte.ed.gov/employabilityskills/) that lists its version of soft skills. OCTAE categorizes its skills into three groupings:

1. Applied knowledge (critical thinking and applied academics)
2. Effective Relationships (interpersonal skills and personal qualities) and
3. Workplace Skills (resource management, information use, communication skills, systems thinking, and technology use).

This set of skills was compiled from numerous resources (http://cte.ed.gov/employabilityskills.index.php/framework/source_matrix) familiar to CTE educators. Most recently, skills in the areas of resource utilization, including categories like time and material management have been added to the Workplace Framework. Also added was financial literacy, including income, expenses, salaries, and benefits.

The importance of these types of skills for employability cannot be overstated. How can educators teach these skills to students? All lesson plans, units, and projects need to incorporate opportunities to encourage, demonstrate, mentor, reflect, and provide feedback to students as they learn and practice targeted skills such as those on the Lesson Planning Checklist of OCTAE (2016). Don't try to incorporate these skills for every lesson, but be sure to model them for your students every day. Think about which one is most important for each lesson or project—

and then focus on it. As you (and your students) become more comfortable with incorporating each soft skill into lessons and projects, teaching those skills should become easier. Remember to ask other teachers and school administrators to share their ideas as to how they teach and encourage students to develop their soft skills.

Collaboration is an important non-cognitive or soft skill for CTE students to learn first. If modeled, encouraged, and supervised positively, it can result in these benefits:

- Improving the end result of a project
- Fostering shared responsibility

- Encouraging peers to challenge one another
- Fostering critical thinking
- Deepening understanding of a specific topic
- Improving learning outcomes, and
- Broadening the understanding of a variety of topics (Greenberg, A., Apr. 2015)

Some other soft skills to be taught could include how to write professional email communications, proper phone etiquette, important customer service communication skills, and timely follow-up and task completion. CTE teachers can promote these highly sought skills by:

- Requiring professional behaviors in the classroom/lab/workshop
- Modeling appropriate interpersonal skills with students and peers
- Designing lessons that incorporate teamwork and problem-solving activities
- Using case studies to examine the impact of ethical behaviors and positive/negative attitudes
- Providing opportunities for students to complete an inventory of their skills and attitudes early in the semester and repeating the measure at the end of the course
- Inviting professionals in your industry or occupational advisory committee (OAC) members to share with your students what they expect of their employees and how to improve their competitive advantage when applying for jobs
- Being an example of life-long learning and discussing why it is important to embrace continuous learning for lifetime success (Philpot, 2010)

Tools For Your Toolbox

As a template for the kinds of standards and competencies involved in workplace readiness, we provide the 21st Century Skills for Workplace Success blueprint. Compiled by NOCTI, it is a nationally-validated list developed with input from national leaders in both industry and education. Its foundation uses a collection of national research and standards from over 20 states. It encompasses historical research dating back to the Secretary's Commission on Necessary Skills (SCANS) and aligns with OCTAE's employability skills framework. The following three areas, Reading, Math and Writing Skills are categorized as academic skills, while the others typically are thought of as employability skills.

Reading Skills

- Interpret and comprehend technical and general written material
- Apply understanding of the material to job tasks

Math Skills

- Perform math operations using whole numbers, fractions, and percentages
- Use statistics (mean, mode, median, standard deviation) to monitor processes and quality of performance
- Use mathematical reasoning to solve word problems and interpret graphics
- Use algebra-based formulas

Writing Skills

- Determine purpose and audience
- Gather information
- Plan the format/layout
- Write a first draft
- Edit and revise to ensure document is complete, clear, concise, correct, courteous, and coherent

Speaking and Listening Skills

- Use effective communication skills
- Provide and comprehend directions or instructions
- Present, and respond to oral reports or presentations
- Participate in group or team discussions
- Engage in conversations with coworkers, supervisors, and clients

Computer Applications and Digital Media

- Utilize word processing, spreadsheet, and database software
- Transfer the operating principles of one application to another similar application
- Use knowledge of computer logic, operating systems, and basic troubleshooting techniques
- Use social media appropriately and effectively, in personal and professional situations

Reasoning, Problem-Solving, and Decision Making

- Differentiate among types of problems (technical, human relations, ethical)
- Use established methods of problem-solving and decision-making in individual and group settings

- Apply previous learning to situations where problems must be solved or decisions made quickly
- Test solutions or decisions to determine effects or to identify related problems

Understanding the "Big Picture"

- Identify the company's mission and the individual employee's contribution to that mission
- Identify how the company functions within the broad world of business, industry, and service
- Interpret organizational policies and procedures
- Explain the necessity and benefits/disadvantages of organizational change
- Explain basic economic concepts

Work Ethics

- Exhibit responsibility
- Exhibit professional practices
- Explain basic legal and fiduciary obligations

Positive Attitude

- Cooperate in a pleasant and polite manner with clients, coworkers, and supervisors
- Exhibit flexibility and adaptability
- Take directions willingly

Independence and Initiative

- Work without constant supervision
- Exhibit willingness to learn
- Find tasks to perform on one's own
- Exhibit interest in making the organization more effective and productive
- Maintain work standards in the midst of change

Self-Presentation

- Identify ways in which the individual employee represents the organization
- Exhibit a neat appearance
- Exhibit elements required in professional settings

Attendance

- Limit tardiness, early departures, and absences to legitimate and essential occasions

- Explain the importance of satisfactory attendance to the overall operation of the business
- Negotiate anticipated absences according to company policy
- Call in to notify the supervisor of unanticipated absences

Collaboration

- Attend team meetings, focus on the topic/purpose, offer facts and ideas, and help others to contribute
- Look for ways to help others
- Recognize others for their contributions
- Let others know what is needed to get the job done
- Provide clear documentation of assignments, goals, and timelines
- Explain the importance of teamwork to the overall operation of the business

Personal Health and Wellness

- Identify healthy practices and behaviors that will maintain or improve personal health
- Identify ways to reduce or prevent injuries and illness

Entrepreneurship

- Identify the characteristics of a successful entrepreneur
- List the advantages and disadvantages of being an entrepreneur
- Identify aspects of owning or starting up a small business

Personal Finance

- Calculate, track, and evaluate income and spending
- Evaluate savings and investment options to meet short and long-term goals
- Analyze the costs and benefits of various types of credit and debt
- Identify and evaluate types of risk and insurance

Our second entry comes from an Illinois WIOA site (Illinois WorkNet), and it discusses the need for these skills from a workforce development agency standpoint:

To succeed in the workplace, it is important to continue to enhance academic skills, technical skills, and workplace soft skills, all of which are gained through experience and training. Often, employers provide additional technical training, but it is up to the individual to demonstrate that they have these skills, such as a good work ethic and a great attitude.

These skills play a vital role when applying for a job and maintaining that job once you are hired, regardless of if you are starting your first job or advancing in your career. These are the skills employers in Illinois require.

Examples of soft/workplace skills include:

- Starting work on time (attendance)
- Dressing properly for work (self-presentation)
- Knowing how to use equipment at work (technical skills)
- Treating others with respect or treating them how you want to be treated (teamwork)
- Having a positive can-do attitude (initiative/positive attitude)
- Using social media (digital literacy/computer skills)
- Making decisions (big picture)
- Writing a journal (communication)
- Fulfilling responsibilities (work ethic), and
- Working on repairing items (problem solving skills)

It is important to:

- Learn about required workplace skills
- Identify the skills you have to offer and the skills you need to improve
- Be able to tell employers about your skills and how they relate to the job for which you are applying

Illinois workNet provides a variety of tools to help individuals enhance their workplace skills. These include the following tools:

- **Illinois workNet Job Skill Guide:** (http://www.illinoisworknet.com/Qualify/Pages/JobSkillsGuides.aspx)
- **Illinois workNet Digital Literacy Guide:** (http://www.illinoisworknet.com/Qualify/Pages/ComputerSkills.aspx)
- **Employment 101 Guide:** Employment 101 is a guided approach that includes assessments, articles, planners, and other resources to help customers reach their training and employment goals.
- **MAPP Career Test** (Assessment.com, 2016) helps gain insights into the careers and the top ten areas with the best fit for an individual.
- **NOCTI 21st Century Skills for Workplace Success Assessment:** The NOCTI 21st Century Skills for Workplace Success Assessment is a non-occupation-specific assessment used to measure employability areas identified in the National Career Cluster model. The results can help customers identify their current skill level and skills that need enhancement.

- **Observational Evaluation:** Training providers use this tool to give customers feedback about their workplace skills using an approach that is similar to one used by an employer. This assessment was developed for use in a program where a person's skills are observed multiple times in different situations over a course of time (six-week minimum is recommended). This ensures that a skillset is habitual, rather than a temporary performance.
- **Worksite Evaluation:** Worksite supervisors use this tool to give interns and youth feedback about their workplace skills while on the job. This assessment was developed for use to provide formative feedback for workers with minimal work experience. A worker's skills are observed multiple times in different situations during the course of their work experience. This is ideal for employers (both work-based learning and job placements) to provide constructive feedback available to workforce partners and the worker.

KEY LEARNINGS:

1. Employability skills are known by many names.
2. Businesses want workers with employability skills.
3. Communication, collaboration, and teamwork are often identified as employment requirements.
4. Decision-making, leadership, and problem solving are frequently included as requirements.
5. Resource management and financial literacy have recently been included in the federal Employability Skills Framework.
6. CTE teachers should model soft skills.
7. CTE teachers should weave opportunities for development of employability skills into their lessons.
8. Students can benefit in the classroom by hearing employers' perspectives on soft skills.

RELATED CONTENT THAT MAY BE OF INTEREST:

American Management Association. (2010). *AMA 2010 Critical Skills Survey*. Available at http://www.amanet.org/

Assessment.com. (2016). *Career Test for High School Students. Career Test for College Students (MAPP Career Test)*. Available at http://www.assessment.com/Students-Graduates.asp.

Employment and Training Administration. (2016, February 25). Competency Models. Available at https://www.doleta.gov/usworkforce/uswf_nav.cfm#Competency.

Greenberg, A., & Nilssen, A. (2015, April). The role of education in building soft skills. *Wainhouse Research*, LLC. Available at cp.wainhouse.com/content/role-education-building-soft-skills.

Hodge, K., & Lear, J. (2011). Employment skills for 21st century workplace: the gap between faculty and student perceptions. *Journal of Career and Technical Education*. 26(2), Available at ejournals.lib.vt.edu.

McKay, D. (2015, November 24). Soft skills: what they are and why you need them. *About.com*. Available at www.careerplanning.about.com.

MindTools. (1996-2016). Why soft skills matter: making sure your hard skills shine. Available at https://www.mindtools.com/pages/article/newCDV_34.htm.

National Association of Colleges and Employers (NACE). (2016). Career Readiness Defined: NACE defines career readiness, identifies key competencies. Available at http://www.naceweb.org/knowledge/career-readiness-competencies.aspx.

Neves, A. (2016). 5 skills you need to work on to get ahead—no matter what industry you're in. *Daily Muse*. Available at https://www.themuse.com/advice/5-skills-you-need-to-work-on-to-get-aheadno-matter-what-industry-youre-in.

Office of Career Technical and Adult Education (OCTAE). (2016). Employability Skills Framework. Washington, DC: U.S. Department of Education. Available at http://cte.ed.gov/employabilityskills/.

Office of Career Technical and Adult Education (OCTAE). (2016). *Lesson Planning Checklist*. Washington, DC: U.S. Department of Education. Available at http://cte.ed.gov/employabilityskills/index.php/developingskills/create_checklist.

Partnership for 21st Century Skills (P21). (2016). Framework for 21st Century Learning. Available at http://www.p21.org/our-work/p21-framework.

RELATED CONTENT THAT MAY BE OF INTEREST, continued:

Philpot, D. (2010, October 27). Soft skills: more important than you might think! *Texas Education Agency, Career and Technical Education Blog*. Available at http://cte-unt.blogspot.com/2010/10/soft-skills-more-important-than-you.html.

Skills You Need Newsletter. (2011-2016). What Are Soft Skills? Available at http://www.skillsyouneed.com/general/soft-skills.html.

The National Career Development Association. (2016). *Internet Sites for Career Planning*. Available at www.ncda.org/aws/NCDA/pt/sp/resources.

chapter VIII
Your Part in Your Students' Futures
Stand by Your Man (or Woman)

In one of our earlier chapters, we talked about accountability and evaluation, and we mentioned that one of the mechanisms for program evaluation (and, sometimes, teacher evaluations) involves student outcome data. Part of a recent federal initiative, Race-To-The-Top (RTTT), called for states to submit teacher evaluation plans, and prioritized the inclusion of student outcome data in teachers' annual evaluations. Even during past iterations of Perkins, most states implemented a student follow-up system that included several basic categories:

1. Employed
2. Pursuing post-secondary education or apprenticeship
3. Enlisted in the military, or
4. Unemployed.

These examples all related to the relationship between teachers and their students, but it was about a relationship governed by regulatory requirements. This chapter discusses that relationship from a different perspective—namely that of teachers as mentors and career advisors for their students.

As we've mentioned numerous times in our books, CTE teachers typically have the benefit of spending a lot of time with their students. Their daily classes are usually longer than other classes, and their time with these same students may cover two to four years. On top of that, most of the time a CTE teacher has fewer students in a given class. Add these benefits up and you have the opportunity to get to know students' personalities, their skills, and their competencies. Research shows that these are elements of a school culture that positively impact students, especially for building characteristics like "grit" and resilience (Krovetz, 2016).

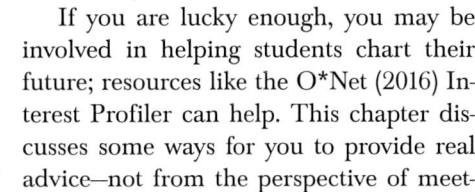

If you are lucky enough, you may be involved in helping students chart their future; resources like the O*Net (2016) Interest Profiler can help. This chapter discusses some ways for you to provide real advice—not from the perspective of meeting a regulatory requirement—but from that of one human being helping another find their way. It's about giving your students that edge in whatever path they choose.

The regulatory reporting requirements mentioned above are general, but can serve as a good method of categorizing the help that a CTE teacher can provide. Those categories could be adapted to pursuing a job (either within a student's CTE pathway or moving outside a CTE pathway), acquiring post-secondary credentials, and following a military route.

Pursuing a Job Within a Student's CTE Pathway

It would be nice to think that students who wanted to become engineers, for example, never veered from their originally chosen path. Life, however, rarely moves down such a straight line. Students who choose to pursue a particular technical specialty may change their minds about their pathway for more reasons than there is space available to list them. This section delineates a few of the advantages a knowledgeable CTE teacher can provide for the student who has chosen to stay in the field. The most common advantage, and probably the best one, for students staying in their chosen field, is finding employment experience before they leave your program. A list of several tools at the end of this chapter can be used by you and your students to explore certifications and career interests.

Students who participate in work-based learning programs have added an in-depth element to their education that school-based learning can never duplicate (ACTE, 2016). Within a work-based learning program, such as an apprenticeship, students are placed into a real-world work situation to further apply and enhance the skills and knowledge learned in your program.

These programs also provide other benefits to students, such as allowing them to discover additional interests and abilities within their content area, while learning about the general responsibilities of any job. They may get the opportunity to work with new equipment and processes, and these experiences may ease the transition from school to work. Of course, the ability to "earn while they learn" is always popular as well.

What can you do to provide this advantage to your students? You can start by assuring employers that you know your students' skills and abilities and know whether or not a work-based learning situation is something in which a given individual would be interested in. Placement in a work-based learning program is generally something that takes time to develop; it relies on networks of people who know employers who are looking for employees. This need can be based on an employer obtaining a new set of customers or clients, turnover from retiring employees, or maybe simply a desire to expand.

A good place to start to inquire about these placements is through your business partners. Your partners may have needs themselves, but just as importantly, they may know of others in the surrounding area that also have needs.

Another approach may lie in an employer's need for finding competent and dedicated employees. Work-based programs provide great opportu-

nities for industry/employers to partner with educators in assisting them in developing future employees. Business and industry personnel may see this as a way to better connect with schools and to share what they feel are the needs of their future employees. Work-based programs may also assist with providing an avenue for business and industry personnel to contribute to the educational process. The final result is the improvement of the connection between the school, community, business, and industry, and in building a trusted network—something any CTE professional should value.

One last employer approach may be the "try before you buy" approach. Placement of a student in work-based learning, particularly a cooperative education placement, provides the employer with an opportunity to see how a student performs in this particular place of business (PA Department of Education, 2014). This approach can work well at times when employers are in your facility during student hours. The employer can see work habits firsthand. This is especially effective if your program participates in an end-of-program performance assessment.

Besides workplace-learning placements, often other opportunities can provide your students with similar kinds of experience. School-based enterprises are opportunities to have customers interact with students in which the school mimics the workplace. Examples can be found in school restaurants, dental clinics, and hair salons. In addition, products may be bought and sold from programs like horticulture, welding, and cabinetmaking. These experiences may provide students the opportunity to hone skills like customer interaction and self- direction. Other skills gained are discussed in the chapter that mentions student-led experiences like West Virginia's "Simulated Workplace."

Working Outside Your CTE Pathway

You'll find that even though you have made a personal commitment to your field of technical expertise, all of your students may not have made that same commitment. Early in your CTE teaching experience, you might think of that as a failure on your part—don't! Sometimes finding out what you don't want to do is almost as important as finding out what you want to do. Everyone has heard stories about individuals with aspirations of becoming medical specialists. They struggle to get through a pre-med course, only to find out that they can't stomach the sight of someone else's blood, or perhaps they had no real perception of the workload and the lifestyle required. Aside from the technical expertise that students can gain from participating in your program, there are some real added real benefits.

As a CTE professional, it's important that you take time to stress those benefits throughout your time with your students. Take time to capitalize on the commonalities and expectations of the workplace that you are providing. Discuss things like cooperation, responsibility, and your part in the bigger picture. You can find a deeper discussion about the employability skills you provide in Chapter VII of this book.

As you look across the various clusters of technical occupations, you can also see some cross-cutting skills. Think about the importance of be-

ing able to read and interpret a technical manual, a blueprint, or a schematic. How many programs are there that cover issues like workplace safety or the importance of sanitary procedures. The career cluster initiative has identified many of these cross-cutting skills, and you can peruse them at Advance CTE (https://careertech.org/). Take time to emphasize how the skills and knowledge you have imparted can apply to areas outside your specific specialty.

Acquiring Postsecondary Credentials

General statistics are plentiful indicating that the higher the degree you are able to acquire, the higher your salary will tend to be (Nunn, 2016). It is important to convey to your students the expectations and advantage of post-secondary credentials in your field. This section focuses on helping students acquire two types of credentials: those that are earned from industry—usually individual companies or industry associations, and those that are derived from community and technical colleges and/or colleges or universities. Each has its own value; a combination of the expectations in your region, as well as perceived market return, will drive that value.

According to the Brookings Institute (Holzer, 2015), middle-skill jobs that continue to pay well are those that require reasoning or communications skills that are not easily replicated by machines. Your students should be aware of the demand for middle-skill jobs that require post-secondary education or a job-related credential or training, such as jobs in healthcare, or mechanical maintenance and repair. Due to the relationships you've developed, you should have a sense of which students have an interest and/or desire to continue their technical training.

Be sure to make your students aware of any industry credentials that may have value in the marketplace. Because of the sheer number and diversity of these credentials (some experts say as many as 6,000 nationally), they cannot be listed in this chapter, but some are listed in a tool at the chapter's end, which lists credentials provided by the National Association of Home Builders (NAHB), the Manufacturing Skills Standards Council (MSSC), and the American Culinary Federation (ACF).

Another advantage for many CTE students is dual-credit programs or articulation agreements. Dual-credit opportunities take a variety of forms, but essentially translate to a secondary student getting credit for a college course and a high school course at the same time. This could mean that a student's secondary teacher has the authority (obtained by the community college) to deliver postsecondary content or that a post-secondary teacher can deliver secondary content. These programs could occur at a secondary site, a postsecondary site, or a neutral site. The combinations are many, but 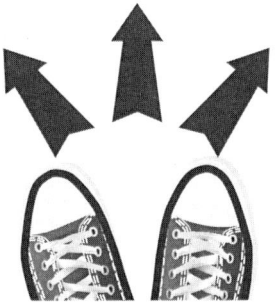 if your school program is involved in dual-credit options, teachers should certainly advocate them to their students.

In an effort to avoid duplication of content for students moving from the secondary to the post-secondary level, many programs are also involved in articulation agreements. These agreements require a level of competence at the secondary level and translate that competence to post-secondary credit or the ability to progress faster through postsecondary content. Sometimes this level of competence is gauged by a third-party analysis (an assessment through an organization like NOCTI) or through a local agreement based on an analysis of content. It can also be accomplished through a statewide agreement, such as the Students Occupationally and Academically Ready (SOAR) program of the PA Department of Education (2013) that prepares students for high-priority occupations and offers incentives to continue educationally. If these opportunities exist, it is your responsibility to make sure your students benefit from them.

Your school may have similar agreements regarding specific employers, apprenticeship programs, and/or your students may have options for testing out of certain postsecondary courses. Digital badges are a potential advantage discussed in the last chapter of this book. All of these are options that you should understand and present as options for your students.

Following a Military Path

CTE teachers sometimes overlook educational and career opportunities in the military that are directly aligned to their instructional programs and which are available to students. This is understandable, because the military is not normally thought of as a CTE customer. The military is generally not considered part of the local labor market, and service members rarely serve on occupational advisory committees. Clearly, CTE teachers support the military and are proud of their students' successes and service in the armed forces, but educators may not promote military services because many are not experts on the many career-training opportunities in the military that are directly related to their subject area. A link to the job titles offered by the U.S. Army is given at the chapter's end.

The military is a major employer in regions that are home to military installations and bases, as the base employs significant numbers of local people working at the base or providing support services to the military. Large numbers of military families live on the base or in the area, and they are part of the local community and schools. Military bases and installations are an important part of the local community, and economic development and the labor market are greatly influenced by their presence.

CTE teachers who have prior military service on active duty or in the National Guard or reserve can relate their first-hand experiences to their students. They can talk about the education and training they received and the career opportunities available to them during their military service. They can tell their students about the ways they applied their civilian and military education during their military career and how the service influenced their career.

Teachers who did not serve in the military can bring knowledge of military service to the classroom by inviting former students who currently serve in the military to relate their experiences to students. Teachers can also invite fellow teachers who served in the military and/or engage military recruiters who frequent the school during career fairs to address students on opportunities related to the CTE subject or occupation. Regardless of who provides the information about education and training options, the message to students should focus on the career opportunities and advantages of military service.

Military service members apply their skills and knowledge as part of a team or military unit, very similar to jobs in business and industry. In most cases, job titles in the military and in industry are the same, and skills and knowledge are applicable to both. In reality, nearly every CTE occupational program is available and essential in the various branches of the military, and CTE students excel in military education and job assignments. Some CTE graduates qualify for advanced standing in military training and receive a higher rank and pay when they report to their job after training.

The formal military education and on-the-job experiences, along with the leadership traits and work ethic that are developed in military service, are very attractive to civilian employers and offer a clear market advantage for military veterans. Veterans typically are very dependable; they possess high technical expertise and often have supervisory experience.

The military creates leadership and supervisory opportunities for young people that would normally not be available in civilian business and industry until they are employed for a much longer period. In addition, veterans of military service, including service in the National Guard and reserve, qualify for college tuition benefits; many colleges provide college credits for skills and knowledge learned while serving in the armed forces.

Although the performance indicators for our schools and programs include placement in the military, it is generally a small percentage of graduates. Yet it is a viable option for every CTE student in pursuit of a technical career. The ever-changing nature of careers and career advancement in the military may make it difficult to know if CTE graduates are serving in military jobs that are directly related to their occupational area in CTE; therefore, the most reliable source of information comes from the personal communications between CTE teachers and their graduates serving in the military. That information should be shared with current CTE students.

For many CTE students, military service offers an ideal career path that provides education and training opportunities that are career enhancing. Students choosing military service take pride in their service to our country, and many experience a different lifestyle that supports their individual and professional growth. Regardless of the length of service chosen, whether it is six months or thirty years, military service includes formal technical training and educational benefits during and after service. CTE teachers should inform their students about all career paths related to their occupational area and assist their students in assessing military options in support of their chosen career.

Tools For Your Toolbox

The first entry in the *Tools* section for this chapter comes from a welding program in Kansas. It shows the importance of planning and collaboration when establishing workplace opportunities:

When I was first teaching in a welding program, I had a chance to set up a work-based learning program. My thought was that if I could get these students some "real-world experience," it would be very beneficial to them. I visited a number of local welding shops and asked them if they would like to have an intern for the summer. Several took me up on this, and I was able to place all my students in a work-based learning situation for the summer. I was very surprised by the outcomes, however! Most of these students had a less than positive experience because they ended up just being a "go-for" or "clean-up person" in these shops. I had failed to make it clear with these shop owners/operators what the learning objectives were for these students.

The following summer, we developed training plans for each student as to what additional things each needed to learn in the welding industry, and then I assisted in matching them up with several welding shops. We formalized the process a bit more and had students apply and interview for the position. We also shared the training plan with the employer. It was then clear to the employer what additional skills the student was seeking to learn, so whoever supervised this student knew what jobs to assign them to fulfill that training plan.

The second summer outcomes were completely different from the first summer. Students and employers both had positive experiences. I learned, as a teacher, that just because you mix students and employers, this does not automatically make a good learning experience. But if it is planned out and both the employer and the student know what is expected of them, then it is more likely to have a positive outcome for all parties involved.

Our second installment is a template for a cooperative education or internship placement:

Big City Schools Cooperative Education
Employer/Student Training Agreement

Student Information

Name: _____

Major: _____

Address: _____

City, State, and Zip: _____

Student ID#: _____

Birth date: _____

Phone #: _____

Cell Phone #: _____

Employer Information

Company Name: _____

Address: _____

City, State, and Zip: _____

Supervisor Name and Title: _____

Phone #: _____

Student Training Period

From: _____ To: _____

Student Beginning Wage

Starting Wage: _____

All should read and agree to the following responsibilities:

Student: I agree to perform all duties as assigned to the best of my abilities; to satisfactorily meet all requirements of the employer and Big City School; and abide by the rules, regulations, and policies of the employer and Big City School. Should I fail to meet these requirements, I may be withdrawn from the Cooperative Education/Internship program and forfeit any academic credits awarded by participation in the program.

Student Signature   Date

_____   _____

Employer: I agree to coordinate the student's work duties so that these duties will be closely related to the student's degree program and career objectives; supervise the student; evaluate the student with forms provided by faculty/coordinator; provide the student the same consideration of health, safety, and working conditions afforded to other full-time employees; and not to discriminate on the basis of race, color, national origin, sex, or handicap.

Employer Signature   Date

_____   _____

Faculty Coordinator: As a representative of Big City School, I agree to maintain communication with the employer and student in an effort to answer questions, resolve potential problems, and strive to make the cooperative education/internship program as productive and rewarding as possible for both the student and employer.

Faculty Coordinator Signature   Date

_____   _____

Our final contribution comes to us from an administrator in Pennsylvania who describes how dual-credit options benefit students wishing to acquire additional post-secondary technical training:

Since 1997, our Technical Institute has offered the Accelerated Career Education System (ACES) in partnership with a local community college. Recognizing high quality education at the secondary level, the ACES provides an opportunity for students to earn as many as 30 college credits for technical assessments (NOCTI and other industry credentials). ACES graduates can continue their studies at the post-secondary level by enrolling in an Associate of Applied Science (A.A.S.) degree program. Beyond the associate degree, students can earn a bachelor's degree offered through a partnership between the community college and a nearby university. Many ACES students can complete their bachelor's degree in three years.

CTE at this center is focused on "High Value" industry certifications and statewide Program of Study (POS) curricula (where available). Student completers take the end-of-program NOCTI credential specific to their CTE program. Additionally, students have an opportunity to earn an additional program-specific industry certification.

When designing the ACES, partners created the A.A.S. in Applied Technical Studies degree at the community college. Articulation agreements were developed with secondary CTE programs that did not have a program-specific associate degree program option available. By doing so, these graduates were provided with an opportunity to earn an associate degree related to their field of study. Additionally, the partners selected programs that were affiliated with a national accreditation body or credentialing organization.

ACES programs at the school included:

- Auto Body Technology
- Automotive Technology
- Carpentry
- Cosmetology
- Culinary Arts
- Diesel Medium/Heavy Truck Technology
- Precision Machine Tool Technology
- Printing Graphic Arts
- Welding Technology

While in high school, ACES students complete their program curriculum, demonstrate mastery of CTE content by earning an average grade of B or higher, and take an end-of-program NOCTI assessment credential specific to their career field. After students have completed one, three-credit non-remedial college course, post-secondary ACES students automatically earn 12 technical college credits. In addition, students are awarded an additional 18 technical college credits for earning specific national certifications (e.g. NATEF/ASE, NIMS, AWS, etc.) as listed in the articulation agreements. These college credits are awarded at no cost, based upon demonstrated student achievement.

The ACES partnership continues to provide a pathway for secondary CTE graduates to link their secondary achievements to a post-secondary opportunity and continue their process of lifelong learning. Students enrolled in the ACES have a head start on their career journey when they graduate high school and begin their post-secondary education.

KEY LEARNINGS:

1. You play an important role in students' futures.
2. Work-based learning opportunities are based on trusted networks.
3. Work-based learning provides employers with a low-risk opportunity to secure technical talent.
4. CTE provides transferable skills; identify them for your students.
5. Post-secondary credentials include employer certifications, as well as college degrees and certificates.
6. Investigate available options for dual credit and articulation in your area and state.
7. The military is a large employer and source of career training.
8. Transferable skills, combined with leadership opportunities, can be earned while serving your country.

RELATED CONTENT THAT MAY BE OF INTEREST:

ACTE. (2016, July). *Leveraging Intermediaries to Expand Work Based Learning.* Available at https://careertech.org/sites/default/files/files/resources/WBL_casestudy_Intermediaries_FINAL.pdf.

American Culinary Federation. (2016). Certify. Available at www.acf-chefs.org/ACF/Certify.

Foster, J.C., Foster, P., Hornberger, C. & McNally, K. (2015). *Your First Year in CTE: 10 More Things to Know.* Alexandria, VA: ACTE.

Holzer, H. (2015, April). *Job Market Polarization and U.S. Worker Skills: A Tale of Two Middles.* Washington, DC: The Brookings Institution. Available at https://www.brookings.edu/research/job-market-polarization-and-u-s-worker-skills-a-tale-of-two-middles/.

RELATED CONTENT THAT MAY BE OF INTEREST, continued:

Kansas State Department of Education. (2013, Sept). *Resource List of Industry-Recognized Assessments/Certifications/Credentials*. Available at http://www.ksde.org/Portals/0/CSAS/CSAS%20Home/CTE%20Home/ Career_Cluster_Pathway/Industry%20Cert%20Resource%20List%20 9-11-13.pdf?ver=2013-09-11-104018-430

Krovetz, M. (2016, March). Expecting all students and educators to use the hearts and minds ell. *Educational Leadership and Administration: Teaching and Program Development*, v27 pp 231-242. ERIC Number: EJ1094429.

Manufacturing Skills Standards Council. (2016). *Manufacturing Skill Standards Certification (MSSC) For Employers*. Kenosha, WI: Author. Available at https://www.gtc.edu/business-workforce-solutions/certifications/mssc.

National Association of Home Builders. (2016). *Course Overviews*. Available at http://www.nahb.org/en/learn/course-overviews.aspx.

Nunn, R. (2016, June 21). *Occupational Licensing and the American Worker*. Washington, DC: The Brookings Institution. Available at https://www.brookings.edu/research/occupational-licensing-and-the-american-worker/.

O*Net. (2016). O*Net Interest Profiler. Washington, DC: U.S. Department of Labor. Available at http://www.mynextmove.org/explore/ip.

PA Department of Education. (2013). SOAR Flyer. Harrisburg, PA: Author. Available at http://www.education.pa.gov/Documents/K-12/Career%20 and%20Technical%20Education/Programs%20of%20Study/SOAR%20 Flyer.pdf.

PA Department of Education. (2014). *Cooperative Education Guidelines for Administration: How to Comply with Federal and State Laws and Regulations*. Harrisburg, PA: Author. http://www.education.pa.gov/ Documents/K-12/Career%20and%20Technical%20Education/Teacher%20Resources/Cooperative%20Education/How%20to%20Comply%20 with%20Federal%20and%20State%20Laws%20and%20Regulations.pdf.

The College Foundation of West Virginia. (2016). *Career Planning*. Charleston, WV: Author. Available at https://www.cfwv.com/Career_Planning/_default.aspx.

West Virginia Department of Education. (2016). Teacher resources. Charleston, WV: Author. Available at http://wvde.state.wv.us/counselors/ links/curriculum/delivery-resources.html.

West Virginia Department of Education. (2016). *Learning, Individualized Needs, Knowledge and Skills (The LINKS program)*. Charleston, WV: Author Available at http://wvde.state.wv.us/counselors/links/about.html

U.S. Army. (2016). U.S. Army Careers and Jobs. Washington, DC: Author. Available at http://www.goarmy.com/careers-and-jobs.html.

chapter IX

Becoming a Leader

I'm the Big Cheese!

During lunch, Mr. Neuteach overheard Ms. Knoscore sharing with other teachers about how proud she was of the students who competed in the recent regional career technical competition. As a CTSO advisor, she talked about how much work went into helping her students prepare for that competition, but she also shared the fun, positive experiences they had and the opportunities that would now be available to her students.

Mr. Neuteach commented that one of those students was his, and he related how excited the student was upon returning from that competition.

Ms. Knoscore smiled and said, "It's a lot of work to prep these kids, and I sure could use some help to get our next batch of students ready for next year's competition!"

Mr. Neuteach thought for a moment. He remembered the work he had put into his own classroom over the last few years and how that focus had isolated him a bit. He thought helping as a CTSO advisor would give him the opportunity to help other students and maybe make some additional CTE teacher friends. He decided that he was ready to help her—to demonstrate that he was willing to become a leader.

Leadership Roles

Strong leadership is vital in many fields, education-related professions certainly among them. Leadership, although a complex construct of characteristics and behaviors, can be observed, learned, and taught (Wonacott, 2003-2004). Viviano (2012) lists four main leadership traits that teachers, students, parents, and stakeholders want to see in their CTE teachers: honesty, forward looking, inspiring, and competent.

Kuchinke (1999) stated that four factors motivate employees to perform beyond expectations by leaders who develop, intellectually stimulate, and inspire them to work toward a collective purpose, mission, or vision:

1. Charisma earns respect, trust, and confidence for leaders and transmits a strong sense of mission and vision.
2. Through intellectual stimulation, leaders actively encourage employees to question the status quo and to critically examine their own assumptions and beliefs, as well as those of leaders and others.
3. Leaders show individual consideration in personalized attention to every employee's needs so that each feels valued; leaders treat employees differently but equitably, based on their needs.
4. Leaders' inspirational motivation communicates a vision and the confident, optimistic, enthusiastic belief that the vision is attainable.

So how can CTE teachers become leaders too? Most do not see themselves as leaders, but administrators cannot perform the complex job of school leadership alone (Leithwood, Louis, Anderson & Wahlstrom, 2004). Many people sometimes equate leaders and bosses, and in the education world "leader" may translate to "building administrator." It follows then, that because they are not in administrative positions, teachers may not consider themselves leaders.

Leaders in education must possess the same personality traits and behaviors as leaders in business, industry, and government. In addition, exceptional leaders also possess technical expertise in their profession. And almost all administrators rely upon the assistance of the leadership of their teachers, which can be an important catalyst for school improvement (Leithwood, et al., 2004). These leadership roles come in many different forms, such as mentoring new teachers, coaching other CTE educators, and becoming CTSO advisors, association leaders, or CTE administrators.

A majority of CTE teachers enter the teaching profession with many years of industry experience. Chances are, you have held a leadership position prior to becoming a teacher. You may have been a lead technician, shift leader, manager, supervisor, foreman, or you may have owned and operated your own business. Most likely, you are recognized by many as a leader in your occupational area. Your business and industry leadership experience and skills are transferable to the field of education.

As you develop your teaching skills, consider sharing your experiences and successes with other new teachers. Sharing your new skills and knowledge reinforces your professional expertise, and it marks the beginning of your role as a mentor and educational leader.

The numerous benefits to becoming a leader within the school setting often require you to step outside of your comfort zone. If you are comfortable, it sometimes means that you are not growing professionally, or maybe it is a signal that you are ready for the next challenge. To remove yourself from your comfort zone requires that you step outside of your program area.

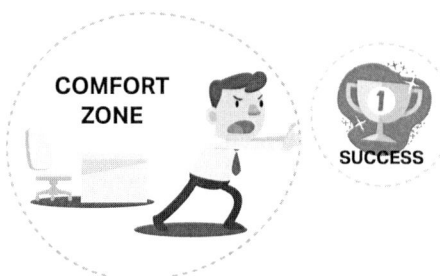

Maybe you could be the one to promote some collegiality in your building by making time to visit other teachers and staff members within your school. This effort can benefit not only those teachers affected, but the entire school environment as well. Another example may be to visit neighboring schools to observe what is working well for their teachers and students and to learn what those schools are doing to demonstrate and promote leadership. A number of states even have statewide content groups, a welding teacher's group, or a nursing teachers' association. These may be great settings in which to demonstrate your leadership abilities.

Within the school system, there are a number of ways to promote leadership. Providing direction for new faculty and staff as a mentor can be an important step toward becoming a leader. Charlotte Danielson (1999) found that mentoring helps novice teachers face their new challenges; through reflective activities and professional conversations, they improve their teaching practices as they assume full responsibility for classes. Well-designed mentoring programs also lower the attrition rates of new teachers (Mordan, 2012); (National Association of State Boards of Education, 1998).

Mentors generally come from two basic areas: non-school-associated (like family and friends) and school-associated. The latter splits into three subgroups:

1. Those in a supervisory role (who provide content expertise, instructional support, classroom management strategies, etc., such as directors, principals, and supervisors) inside the school system.
2. Those who can provide content expertise and up-to-date changes of technical information, procedures, equipment, etc. (such as another teacher who teaches the same career-technical area within the school or at another school, or an OAC member), inside or outside of the school system.
3. Those individuals who help a new teacher to find his or her balance (such as other teachers, instructional support communities, and professional associations), inside or outside of the school system.

For more information about mentors and mentoring, you may want to read Chapter III: "Who's Got Your Back?" in the handbook *Your First Year in CTE: 10 Things to Know* (2014).

Often a new CTE teacher does not come directly from a teacher preparation program. Frequently, he or she has worked in a technical area for several (or many) years and then needs to make the transition to teaching students, initially without the background of a more traditional pedagogy of education courses, student teaching supervision and experiences, and so forth. Unfortunately, too many become overwhelmed within the first three to four years and decide to leave teaching and seek employment again in industry (Mordan, 2012). Effective mentoring aims to increase teacher retention, improve teacher training, enhance teacher effectiveness, and advance student learning.

A type of informal mentoring, one that can also encourage leadership among faculty, can be to develop a peer coaching program. For example, one teacher volunteers to collaborate with another teacher with the goal of improving a chosen instructional strategy or a classroom management concern, whatever each feels that he or she would like to improve. They meet whenever is convenient for both and discuss what each of them

would like to target as areas for improvement in the classroom. They choose a date for the classroom observation(s) and later provide informal, non-threatening feedback concerning the targeted area.

Having another professional in the classroom to observe and provide positive reinforcement and suggestions can provide insight to that a teacher may not otherwise get. And although an administrator may strive to provide that feedback and guidance as well, that usually is conducted on a more formal basis with perceived higher stakes by the teacher. Peer coaching is an opportunity for the teacher to begin to take on a leadership role with fellow teachers in a supportive, non-threatening, collaborative way. It really does not require financial support unless the school district wants to provide some professional development and guidelines for a more formal peer-coaching program.

Many other ways to promote leadership within the school system can be found by serving on professional committees or school improvement or planning committees, participating in teacher associations, unions and bargaining units, becoming a CTSO advisor, assisting other teachers with CTSOs, helping with student fundraisers, or perhaps helping with volunteer events. Rodman (2012) states that involving teachers in planning and implementing brings higher success rates in school reform efforts.

Another opportunity for leadership may exist in the regional education community. Sometimes a physical separation exists between the CTE school and the schools from which CTE students come for part of the day. These schools are typically comprehensive high schools and their staff may not be aware of the educational opportunities at the CTE center. Conversely, those at the CTE center may be unaware of opportunities at the high schools. Helping to bridge this gap is critical, and positive, for both entities, and provides opportunities for leadership.

Leadership and Professional Development

Professional development is a planned activity that aids the CTE teacher in staying current in the teaching profession—but CTE teachers are faced with two challenges in keeping up professionally. One is staying current in their technical content and its changing technology, tools, materials, and procedures; the other is keeping abreast of trends and techniques in general education delivery and technique. Many professional development opportunities available to CTE teachers tend to be driven toward delivery and technique. Perhaps another opportunity for leadership would involve coordinating a technical content update delivered by a practicing technician. You could be that technician with an update in your field of technical expertise. You could also demonstrate leadership by organizing an opportunity where teachers in programs with similar content can share.

As new teachers develop their skills in the classroom, they develop a vision of where they want to be as educational professionals. CTE teachers should prepare a plan for their own professional careers. Mentor teachers and administrators can assist new teachers in gaining a better understanding of the career opportunities in CTE and developing strategies to achieve professional goals. The range of experience and postsecondary education levels among new CTE teachers varies greatly, from no college experience to graduate degrees.

The path to career success will require a wide range of continuous professional development activities, possibly including additional college courses and degrees. The goal for many teachers is to continue to enhance their professional skills in order to become "master teachers." Others may view their career progression beyond the classroom as CTE administrators and leaders. Regardless of the individual career goals of teachers, leadership is essential for success in the classroom and lab or in a supervisory position. All will need to practice leadership skills on a regular basis.

Even though the primary focus on professional development and growth is on the teacher, students should benefit as well. The more knowledgeable the CTE teachers are in their content areas, the more they can share this information, experiences and opportunities with their students. Students who have teachers who have maintained their technical expertise tend to leave the program with additional advanced skills and knowledge, so it is a win-win for all.

The teaching profession needs your leadership! Leaders are important in all settings, and education is no different. You may not consider yourself to be a leader, but you have much to contribute to the teaching profession. Your experience and dedication will assist other teachers as they grow within the profession. Look for opportunities to serve your professional organization within your content area.

Leaders participate in professional learning within and beyond their work environment; they make their career-long learning visible, and they consume information from multiple fields to enhance their leadership practice (Jackson, 2016). A service opportunity is the Career and Technical Teacher organization for your state. Become a member or volunteer to help these organizations. Doing so will not only help to provide direction for the specific organization, it may also help to improve the teaching profession as a whole.

Additionally, at the national level, CTE teachers can participate in the Association of Career and Technical Education (ACTE). Attend state and national conferences on CTE such as the ACTE CareerTech VISION Conference. You can keep current with the profession and subscribe to ACTE's Smart Briefs at www.acteonline.org and the *Techniques* magazine to broaden your knowledge in CTE. Whatever you choose to do, expand your expertise in CTE beyond your school and classroom experience.

All of these examples of leadership opportunities for CTE teachers not only help to benefit the individuals, but they also benefit the education community as a whole. What can YOU do to step up and promote leadership in your school, with your students, your peers, and your community?

Tools For Your Toolbox

Our first entry comes from an experienced retired science teacher/administrator from Pennsylvania who mentored a new precision machine technology teacher who had replaced a prior teacher in the middle of a school year. That mentoring process, from one teacher to another, not only provided immediate assistance to the new teacher but it also planted the seeds of leadership:

> Although the new teacher thought that he would have few discipline problems because his students had elected to participate in his program, he found this not to be true, at least not with all his students. His mentor not only guided him in creating safety procedures, lesson plans, grading, and so forth, but she also helped him to establish firm but fair rules of student conduct and reinforcement. She assisted him in developing guidelines for interacting with students and their parents/guardians. She also provides guidance about the many other facets of teaching teenage students.
>
> The prior teacher had given some of these students high grades on their report cards although they had not completed projects within the set time period. Such would not be the case with the new teacher. Obviously,

some students were resistant to the new teacher's expectations, but by the end of that first school year, most had learned that the new teacher possessed significant knowledge and skills that he would teach them if they did what was expected of them. Students soon realized that their new teacher really cared about them. By the end of the second school year, three of this new teacher's students placed first or second at the State SkillsUSA competition, and one went on to take second place at the national competition!

Having that mentor fulltime in the classroom for the first few weeks and periodically afterward may not be the usual scenario for many new CTE teachers, but it did positively impact the new teacher's transition from industry to the classroom (Mordan, 2012). Learning from the example that was provided to him, that new teacher is now stepping up to become a leader in his school by serving as a mentor for some of the newer teachers. He has been in their shoes and wants to help them to find success in their teaching careers as well.

Our second entry comes from a CTE professor in Kansas who was implementing a software solution for career guidance into a CTE academy. At the conclusion of his experience, he paused to reflect about what he had learned:

It was my responsibility to work with Tech Support to get this system up and running. In doing this, it became evident that this wasn't something we could just "throw out" to staff and expect them to use. I asked to meet with our CTE Director, Assistant Superintendent, High School Lead Counselor, and Curriculum Specialist for K-8 and 9-12. During the meeting, I asked them to share input as to how we could implement this across the district. It was up to me to share everything that we could offer students who would be using the software.

This group put together the leads for each grade level. I began planning short meetings with the appropriate levels. I wanted to make sure I didn't include K-8 levels if the focus of the meetings was more centered for grades 9-12, and vice versa. This was very important because I had attended meetings in the past that left me wondering why I was there. My most active role in working through this process was focused on grade levels 7-12.

The first thing we did was lay out a spreadsheet that showed the activities done at each level to make sure students were not constantly repeating activities and not seeing the value or growth in their plans of study. Once this was established, I worked to find people willing to become trainers in our areas of emphasis. The final steps included working with administration in making sure all our staff received consistent training.

My Reflections:

- Make sure you have the right audience for your activity.
- Meetings to plan meetings are less productive and it is important to be completely prepared before asking involved parties to meet.
- The more information that can be summarized, the more productive meetings will be.
- Put yourself in the other person's shoes.

Our third and final entry for your toolbox consideration is from a large career and technical center's seasoned administrator in Georgia. He provides a brief checklist that can help identify potential leaders, but explains that this is just the first step: Finding a leader in the CTE teaching ranks starts with examining objective evidence from the activities that he/she can create involving opportunities for student success. There are several questions that can be asked to determine leadership in CTE:

- What percentage of students are receiving industry credentials in the program area?
- What percentage of students that are enrolled in the teacher's courses are members in a CTSO?
- How many students compete at regional, state, and national CTSO student leadership conferences?
- How many, and what type, of businesses and industry partners are engaged in the program area?
- What percentage of students entered post-secondary, workforce, military, or advance training programs immediately after high school?

The answer to these few questions will identify CTE teachers with potential to become leaders. As a CTE Director for 19 years in two different school systems, I have seen many qualified and non-qualified teachers apply for leadership positions in public school systems. The most effective CTE leaders have been the ones that have proven themselves with evidence from their classroom experiences. CTE teachers truly appreciate leaders that know what it takes to provide successful strategies for students and program successes.

We know that all teachers want their students to be successful and will follow a leader who has demonstrated success in CTE. Also, CTE teachers that have proven themselves will have credibility with their colleagues, who will be more willing to follow their direction and leadership. When you have walked in the shoes of others, you are able to help followers to become top performers in students' achieving career and college success.

Good CTE teachers must stay connected to research and current issues that impact the work of preparing students for life beyond high school. Membership in professional organizations such as ACTE and specific industry areas is critical for continuous improvements and professional growth. Presenting best practices at a local, state, or national conference is the greatest way to learn. Serving as an officer in a professional organization will allow a CTE leader to gain the experience to assist and support other CTE teachers in implementing new strategies and adjustments to program delivery. Potential CTE teacher leaders can reach out to their current leaders to volunteer to meet a need to improve student academic achievement. Being a team member and developing relationships with colleagues will allow you to gain interpersonal skills to bring people together for improvements and to attain common goals.

KEY LEARNINGS:

1. Leadership is vital.
2. There are many ways to become an educational leader.
3. Consider sharing what has worked in your class-room.
4. Establish a positive rapport with peers.
5. Serve as a mentor.
6. Serve on a professional committee.
7. Plan your professional career.
8. Join your national association.

RELATED CONTENT THAT MAY BE OF INTEREST:

Cole, B., Foster, J., Foster, P., and McNally, K. (2014). *Your First Year in CTE: 10 Things to Know*. Alexandria, VA: Association for Career and Technical Education. Available at www.acteonline.org.

Danielson, C. (1999). Mentoring beginning teachers: The case for mentoring. *Teaching and Change*, 6(3), pp. 251-257.

Jackson, D. (2016). Standards for professional learning. *Learning Forward*. Available at https://learningforward.org/standards/leadership.

Kuchinke, K. (1999). Workforce education faculty as leaders: Do graduate-level university instructors exhibit transformational leadership behaviors? *Journal of Vocational Education Research*, 24(4) pp 209-225.

Leithwood, K., Louis, K. S., Anderson, S., & Wahlstrom, K. (2004). How Leadership Influences Student Learning. Retrieved from http://www.wallacefoundation.org/ knowledge-center/school-leadership/keyresearch/Documents/How-Leadership-Influences-Student-Learning.pdf

Mordan, B.R. (2012, December). *Retention and Professional Mentoring Of Beginning Career and Technical Education Teachers*. Pennsylvania State University. Unpublished dissertation available at https://etda.libraries.psu.edu/files/final_submissions/7966

National Association of State Boards of Education. (1998, October). *The Numbers Game: Ensuring Quantity and Quality in the Teaching Workforce*. The Report of The NASBE Study Group On Teacher Development, Supply, and Demand. Alexandria, VA: Author. Available at http://nasbe.org/wp-content/uploads/SG_Numbers_Game_1_Teacher_Development_1998.pdf

Rodman, M. (2012). *A Study of Learning-Centered Leadership Skills of Principals in Career and Technical Education Schools*. Pennsylvania State University. Unpublished dissertation. Available at https://etda.libraries.psu.edu/files/final_submissions/7033.

Viviano, T. (2012, Winter). What 21st century leadership in career and technical education should look like. *Journal of Career and Technical Education*, 27(2) pp 51-56. EJ995894.

Wonacott, M. (2001). Leadership Development in Career and Technical Education. *ERIC Digest No. 225*. ED452366 2001-00-00. Available at http://eric.ed.gov/.

chapter X

Future Issues

The Future's So Bright ...
I Gotta Wear Shades!

"Better, faster, smaller, cheaper" sounds like an ad for a household product you might see on one of those television shopping networks, right? The reality is that this is an amazing time in education. Actually, it's an amazing time in our history, too. From technology and instructional research to medical research, there are substantial advances almost daily. So, where can a CTE educator focus? In your past life, you focused on materials, processes, products, and new regulations in your particular field. It isn't actually that much different.

This new educational career of yours focuses on making your students as successful as they can be, not on building the best widget. Regardless of the content you deliver, you use that content as a vehicle for delivering deeper learning and a way to make your students competitive in the global job market, so you should take a look at anything that can give them an advantage.

We could devote the entire book to the topic of "future issues." This chapter isn't about selecting 3D printers, lasers, or robots. We chose instead to focus on a few key categories and their connection to your classroom. Our general categories are online resources, personalized learning, credentialing, and employability/entrepreneurship.

Online Learning Resources

Once the World-Wide Web had started to take hold in education circles somewhere around the mid-1990s, we first started to witness a merger of sorts. That merger was between computer learning programs and the web's ability to not only deliver them in multiple places, but to also update them simultaneously for everyone. It provided a means of updating information without the costs of print-based materials.

We saw the development and enhancement of modularized packages that focused on content in small pieces. If you were a Business Education

teacher, perhaps you had a program that explained how to use a particular piece of word processing software that was installed on every computer in your classroom and your students worked through it together. If you were a Technology Education teacher, you might have had several pieces of different software that were installed on different computers in your classroom. You rotated your students through each of them to gain different competencies that related to different technologies (aviation, plastics, rocketry, etc.). Perhaps if you were a Trade and Industrial teacher, you might have had a modular program on OSHA safety regulations that each student had to complete at his or her own pace.

Creative teachers and instructional technologies have obviously progressed in recent years (DiMaria, 2016). Today there is much written about instructional techniques like asynchronous learning (a student-centered learning technique that takes place outside of the restraints of a typical school day); blended classrooms (a combination of teacher-lead instruction combined with digital media instruction, see Patrick & Sturgis, 2015); and the use of open resources found on the web, like MOOCs (Massively Open Online Courses). All of these styles, and others like online subscription-based curricula, are considerations for your classroom. After doing some initial research, you'll need to investigate policies and associated costs at the educational setting in which you work. For example, many auto mechanic programs subscribe to online diagnostic tools and there may be a state subscription to these services.

Generally speaking, online resources, whether subscription-based and password-protected or free and open, provide current resources that are easily updated and may either supplement or supplant a portion of the instruction that you provide to your students. Most CTE facilities have a person dedicated to the schools' IT infrastructure and that individual, or a computer teacher, may be a good place to help you to determine your parameters.

Personalized Learning

CTE has a long history of developing the competencies of an individual. In fact, many researchers credit vocational education as being a significant  part of competency-based education (an educational reform movement from the 1960s which differs from today's version which focuses on having students advance at different rates, based on their ability to demonstrate mastery of learning objectives). It's no surprise then that CTE would be comfortable with the newer forms of personalized learning (Rickabaugh, 2015).

CTE curriculum is based, at some level, on a process known as job task analysis that is widely used in determining job content and job descriptions. This means that a group of experts, either public or private, dissected your particular technical area and divided it into its basic standards and competencies. One of the jobs of the CTE teacher is to deliver these standards and competencies on an individual basis to each student in his or her class. In order to do that, there needs to be some form of individualized progress documentation. Some students may take more time to practice a particular skill and others may take less, so students must be allowed to progress at their own rates to achieve mastery. In the past, this challenged CTE teachers, but with advances in technology, things have become somewhat simpler. A few of the categories are listed below:

Program Of Study (POS): A policy framework required by recent Perkins legislation (Perkins, 2006; NRCCTE, n.d.) that shows a non-duplicative sequence of courses from secondary to post-secondary in a variety of technical fields. This framework is built around sequences of academic and career technical education coursework to help students attain a post-secondary degree or industry-recognized certificate or credential, otherwise known as programs of study (POS).

Online Learning: Earlier in this chapter, we mentioned the explosion of online resources for the CTE classroom. These resources can be specific subscription-based technical curriculum, or they can be free, succinct "how to" videos. Aggregators of specialized content are also starting to appear. Whatever online resource you choose to use, you have the flexibility to assign it to an individual, a group of individuals, or an entire class. Sites like Google docs (https://www.google.com/docs/about/) and others have created platforms where groups of teachers can "crowd source" (resources assembled on a single topic by groups of paid or unpaid individuals).

Electronic Communication: CTE teachers have countless methods of reaching out to their students to communicate on the progress of their learning. Social media sites (e.g., Facebook, Twitter, Snapchat, LinkedIn, Instagram) are all possibilities. Don't forget about methods like e-mailing, texting, and instant messaging as well. Of course, prior to engaging in these forms of education or communication resources, be aware of any policies your district may have in place and remember the cautions in our first book, *Your First Year in CTE: 10 Things to Know*, Chapter V: Sometimes You Have to Build Fences (Cole, 2014). There are a number of platforms available that give students the ability to upload a project to a proprietary site. Their teacher accesses that same site and provides feedback, which the students then download. This creates a continuous improvement process where students can receive individual feedback.

These are just a few examples of personalized learning trends. They may be things you are already doing, things you want to do, or combinations you want to try. Regardless of how you choose to use personalized learning tools, these tools represent ways to extend the learning beyond the school day, design individualized meaningful pathways to success, and enhance the relationship of mentor and guide for the students you serve.

Credentialing

Earlier in this book, and in *Your First Year in CTE: 10 MORE Things to Know*, we discussed aspects of accountability and issues surrounding the importance of reports from a legislative perspective. It is a given that any CTE program must report on the competencies of its students (Perkins, 2006), but how is this being done and how can it be done better?

At the conclusion of any CTE program, there may be an end-of-program assessment. This assessment should be industry-based, valid, and reliable. It may result in a credential of some sort, which represents the expectations of experts in your particular field. These assessments may be given in a computer lab, like any other sort of standardized test. They may have some bells and whistles, like drag and drops or short videos to evaluate.

CTE is all about live performance, yet very few states currently require their students to demonstrate their skills. Performance tests are typically more difficult for schools to implement because of both human and financial resources, so here are some options to consider:

Performance Test Delivery Options: Most CTE graduates need to be evaluated based on process and product; process requires experts using a standardized rubric for each student (or student group) (Robinson, 2016). Can we attest to competency if we only look at product? If we only look at product, and the product was electronically uploaded, we can significantly reduce the costs of evaluation while simultaneously making the evaluation more consistent. Some companies are starting to look seriously at this approach. Simulations and gaming have also been improving, and depending on the occupational specialties (IT, welding, heavy equipment, HVAC troubleshooting, etc.), they may be an option for demonstrating competence.

Monitoring/security options: The typical standardized test scenario involves an individual watching over students in a computer lab. Though numerous controls are being implemented in software itself, some out-of-the-box methods are possible. For example, what if students were allowed to take end-of-program assessments on their own devices? A number of firms are experimenting with this option. What if CTE graduates were allowed to take their assessments at home and they were monitored with webcams and other technologies? Companies like Proctor U (http://www.proctoru.com/howitworks.php) are already partnering with NOCTI to do just that.

Recognition options: Digital recognition (electronic badges or microcredentials) have provided a whole new way to recognize student achievement. Essentially, if a student meets the conditions established by technical  experts on a standardized technical rubric, they are awarded a digital badge. Numerous researchers have talked about badges having the potential to "disrupt the diploma." (Hoffman, 2013; Peck, 2013) The thought is that current educational diplomas and transcripts provide no meaningful information about actual competencies (Robinson, 2016). They represent a collection of subjective grades received from one educational institution. Badges, on the other hand, represent a mechanism to identify specific skill sets that are recognized nationally by groups of experts instead of one individual. More importantly, they recognize a student accomplishment—one that the student can share any place he or she desires. Badge data are available 24/7 and are validated by linking to the exact standards met and the organization that established them.

Employability and Entrepreneurship

It seems that each day an additional state is putting into educational policy the requirement for its students to be career and college ready. The difficulty is in defining what that actually means. The other difficulty is in trying to accomplish that goal.

Much has been written regarding the connection between an individual and the contributions that he or she will make through meaningful work. Futurists have also predicted that, because of increasing automation and human longevity, there may not be enough employment for people to have their own jobs in the future. If part of this prediction becomes a reality, it seems that employability skills (sometimes called workplace skills or soft skills) and entrepreneurial skills may be the answer. Some say that technical skills enable you to enter employment, but it's your employability skills that help you keep that job. (For further information, refer to Chapter VII in this book). Here are a few examples regarding the direction of employability skills:

California: Has established a set of skills called "Standards for Career Ready Practice." These include 21 separate skills, including things like using technology to solve problems," communication skills, and financial literacy skills. (http://www.cde.ca.gov/ci/ct/sf/documents/ctescrpflyer.pdf)

Employment and Training Agency (ETA): In the late 1990s, the Department of Labor's competency modeling initiative began. As part of that program, the ETA developed six tiers of skills that a person needed to secure employment (http://www.careeronestop.org/competencymodel/competency-models/building-blocks-model.aspx). The first three are personal effectiveness competencies, academic competencies, and workplace competencies. These three tiers include things like integrity, initiative, critical and analytic thinking, and planning and organizing.

OCTAE Employability Skills Framework: The U.S. Department of Education also promotes employability skills. Their framework consists of applied knowledge, effective relationships, and workplace skills (http://cte.ed.gov/employabilityskills/). Like the ETA model, there are categories that include information use, resource management, systems thinking, and technology use.

Pennsylvania Career Education and Work Standard: Pennsylvania took a slightly different route, and their standards include areas of knowledge that will be measured during three phases of a student's public education. Those four areas are career awareness and preparation, career acquisition, career retention and advancement, and entrepreneurship. (http://www.pacareerstandards.com/).

Even from this brief description of four sets of employability standards, one can see the commonalities and overlaps between them. Numerous tools exist to measure these competencies, and they are likely to shift in tandem with societal needs.

Entrepreneurship

Type the words "entrepreneurship certification" into a search engine, and you will find hundreds of opportunities to pursue programs and/

or credentials in entrepreneurship. That alone should underscore the importance of these skills. A number of people in the media refer to something called the "underground economy." This is the economy made up of individual inventors, among other things, who follow their passion in developing a product or a service and typically aren't captured in national employment data figures.

If that isn't enough, take a look at sites like Kickstarter (https://www.kickstarter.com), Indiegogo (https://www.indiegogo.com), and others. These sites help provide inventors with crowdfunded monies so they can develop and produce an idea. Can you utilize any of these ideas or sites in your classroom? You can find more ideas by looking into entrepreneurial organizations like the Virtual Enterprises International (http://www.nocti.org/CertificateProgram-VEI.cfm).

As was mentioned at the start of this chapter, an entire book could be dedicated to directions that education is headed, both from a technology standpoint and a policy standpoint. The authors in this chapter hope that your appetite has been whetted for some other things occurring and that you now have some samples of things that you can begin to look into as you enhance your ability to prepare the workforce of tomorrow.

Tools For Your Toolbox

Our first entry in this chapter's *Tools* section is from the International Standards for Technology Educators (ISTE, 2009), and it describes proficiencies needed by all teachers in the 21st Century. Though these standards are broadly focused, they do relate to some of the topics covered in this chapter.

1. Facilitate and inspire student learning and creativity.
2. Design and develop digital-age learning experiences and assessments.
3. Model digital- age work and learning.
4. Promote and model digital citizenship and responsibility.
5. Engage in professional growth and leadership.

These five proficiencies relate to some of the topics covered in this chapter. Creatively using some of the apps for social media to convey information, utilizing online curriculum sources, employing digital badges, and taking advantage of technology-based online professional development options are topics that align with the 21st Century Teacher Proficiencies.

Our second entry comes to us from an enthusiastic early childhood teacher in California. She talks about her experience with digital badging and its benefits from a motivational perspective:

I find the digital badge is a great incentive for student achievement. The students find it beneficial and exciting that once they have earned a badge, they have the opportunity to display it electronically for universities, potential employers, scholarship providers, and to friends on social media. Almost 80% of my students met the criteria established to earn college credit and received a digital badge attesting to it. That badge was not only a source of pride, but it also demonstrated the individual skills and competencies of my students.

Parents and administrators viewed the badge as further validation of a great program here at our Regional Occupational Center (ROP). By compiling the data about my students who participated in the assessment that earned them the badge, I can also see the strengths and weaknesses of a particular class. When I look at this information longitudinally (year after year), it gives me a pretty good idea of my own instructional ability. I hope to be able to use the information to help personalize my instruction as well.

I love the fact that the credentialing test we use (NOCTI) is comprehensive and compares my students with programs all over the U.S.A.

Our final entry is a listing of three websites we thought might be helpful.

1. An alternative to PowerPoint designed for those who like to develop lessons into stories can be found in Prezi. (http://prezi.com)
2. An innovative video-driven design program called VideoScribe may be a great tool for imaginative CTE teachers. (http://www.videoscribe.com)
3. A tool for designing video lessons can be found at Zaption. (https://zaption.zendesk.com/hc/en-us/articles/203066145-Create-a-Lesson-Quick-Video-Tutorial)

KEY LEARNINGS:

1. New technologies and progressive policies impact CTE's future.
2. Online CTE resources are expanding rapidly.
3. Quality online content for CTE can be public or private, free, or costly.
4. Personalized learning meshes well with CTE and its competency-based learning approach.
5. Electronic communication methods can extend the CTE classroom beyond its walls.
6. Digital options for demonstrating CTE performance are increasing.
7. Digital badges fit well with CTE's emphasis on competency.
8. Employment and entrepreneurial skills are needed by your students if they are to stay employed.

RELATED CONTENT THAT MAY BE OF INTEREST:

Bock, S. H. (2010, January). Teacher recognition. *Techniques*. (85) 1, 30-33.

California Department of Education. (n.d.). Standards for Career Ready Practice. Available at http://www.cde.ca.gov/ci/ct/sf/documents/cte-scrpflyer.pdf.

Carl D. Perkins Career and Technical Education Act of 2006 (Perkins IV). (Public Law 109-270).

Cole, B. (2014). Chapter V: Sometimes you have to build fences. In Cole, B., Foster, J., Foster, P. & McNally, K., *Your First Year in CTE: Ten Things to Know,* pp. 32-37. Alexandria, VA: ACTE.

EdWeek Webinar Archive. (2016, March 8). Go Digital with Formative Assessment & Critical Thinking. Available at https://vts.inxpo.com/scripts/Server.nxp?LASCmd=AI:4;F:QS!10100&ShowKey=30157&part nerref=TOC&Referrer=http%3A%2F%2Fwww.edweek.org%2Few%2F marketplace%2Fwebinars%2Fwebinars.html.

DiMaria, F. (2016, April 16). Allowing technology to amplify quality teaching. *THE Journal*. Available at https://thejournal.com/articles/2016/04/20/allowing-technology-to-amplify-quality-teaching.aspx.

Foster, J., Foster, P., Hornberger, C., & McNally, K. (2015). *Your First Year in CTE: 10 MORE Things to Know*. Alexandria, VA: ACTE.

Hoffman, R. (2013, September 16). Disrupting the Diploma. *LinkedIn Pulse*. Available at https://www.linkedin.com/pulse/20130916065028-1213-disrupting-the-diploma.

International Society for Technology in Education (ISTE). (2009). *Digital age leadership, Standards for Teachers*. ISTE standards found at http://www.iste.org/standards/standards/standards-for-teachers.

National Research Center for Career and Technical Education (NRCCTE). (n.d.). Career Pathways and Programs of Study, The National Research Center for Career and Technical Education at the Southern Regional Education Board. Retrieved July 29, 2016 from http://www.nrccte.org/core-issues/programs-study.

Office of Career, Technical, and Adult Education (OCTAE). (n.d.). *OCTAE Employability Skills Framework*. U.S. Department of Education. Available at http://cte.ed.gov/employabilityskills/.

Patrick, S. & Sturgis, C. (2015, March). *Maximizing Competency Education and Blended Learning*. Competency Works Issue Brief. Vienna, VA: International Association for K-12 Online Learning. Available through http://eric.ed.gov/ number ED557755.

RELATED CONTENT THAT MAY BE OF INTEREST, continued:

Peck, K. L. (2013, Fall). Measuring success: Reinventing the report card. AdvancED. Available at http://www.advanc-ed.org/source/reinventing-report-card.

Pennsylvania Department of Education. (n.d.). *Career Education & Work (CEW) Standards Toolkit*, Bureau of Career and Technical Education. Available at http://www.pacareerstandards.com/.

Rickabaugh, J. (2015). Including the learner in personalized learning. *Connect: Making Learning Personal Issue Brief*. Center on Innovations in Learning, Philadelphia, PA: Temple University. Available through http://eric.ed.gov/ ED558048.

Robinson, G. (2016, July 27). Presentations and portfolios take the place of tests for some students. *Hechinger Report*. http://hechinger-report.org/presentations-and-portfolios-take-the-place-of-tests-for-some-students/.

Conclusion

In our *Setting the Stage* introduction, we discussed becoming a professional CTE teacher and reiterated that those entering the field through alternative certification paths are truly a special breed. The numerous differences between these educators and other traditionally-prepared educators include differences in prior work experience, work environments, and knowledge of how to operate a safe learning environment for students. Although there are many books on teaching strategies, with quite a few on tips for new teachers, we are aware of none focused on new CTE teachers who have come primarily from alternative-certification programs, and certainly none that discuss their responsibilities to their profession.

We hope this book, especially when coupled with our other two books, has shed some light on some of the details of becoming a CTE professional. *Your First Year in CTE: 10 Things to Know* focused most heavily on the importance of relationship building, not only with students, but also with peers and supervisors. *Your First Year in CTE: 10 MORE Things to Know* focused on more detailed issues, organized into the importance of planning, assessing, and using external relationships. *Beyond Your First Year in CTE: 10 Additional Things to Know* focuses on what it takes to be a professional educator in CTE.

All three of the books are short, simple, focused but lighthearted resources that focus on helping the new CTE teacher. We maintained the teacher reflections and usable examples from real classrooms called "Tools for Your Toolbox." The *Tools* section is near the end of every chapter (just before *Key Learnings* and *Related Content That May Be of Interest),* and we have included a minimum of three "tools" in each chapter. We would also encourage each of you to think about submitting something to us directly or to post things on ACTE's website that would be of benefit to your peers—kind of a pay-it-forward" approach. Lastly, as we have done with previous chapters and with our last book, we want to provide you a list of key points from the overall book. So, in no particular order, here they are!

- Federal legislation has an impact on your classroom, and you can have an impact on federal legislation. CTE professionals should stay abreast of both regulatory and non-regulatory guidance as it frequently mediates legislative intent and practical implications for CTE classrooms.
- Build your professional network by joining and supporting national organizations. These organizations provide opportunities for networking, professional learning and leadership development.
- Be aware of the variety of options that exist for your students to transition to post-secondary education. A few of these include dual credit, prior learning assessments, and the awarding of college credit for industry credentials.
- One of the most important gifts you can receive from others is the gift of respect. Strive to be a positive influence in the lives of your students.
- Individualized learning, project-based learning, and student-centered learning are all examples of strategies of which a professional CTE educator should be familiar.
- Teacher evaluation has numerous implications for professional growth as well as continued state and federal funding. Get involved and stay positive!
- Technical skill competence helps your students obtain a job, but their employability skills, collaboration, cooperation, and ability to see the big picture are critical to keeping that job. Incorporate those employability skills into your teaching wherever possible.
- You can be the key to your students' future, regardless of their goals. You can help them enter careers that they can access out of your program, that require post-secondary education, that are outside of your specific area of expertise, or that link to employment in the military.
- Become a leader, if you aren't already!
- The future is yours to create, for you and your students. Do your best to stay current with trends in education, technical training, and educational technology.

The authors and the contributing authors really hope you find this book useful and that you will consider placing your "toolbox tools" at ACTE's website found at www.acteonline.org/shopacte!

Contributing
Authors

Edward A. Bouquillon, Ph.D. *(Chapter I)*
Minuteman Regional Vocational Technical High School, Superinten-
dent-Director, Massachusetts

Cynthia Brennan-Jones, Ph.D. *(Chapter VI)*
Indian River State College, Learning Facilitator, Florida

Ed Chipalowsky *(Chapter II)*
Monroe Career and Technical Institute, Diesel Technology Instructor,
Pennsylvania

Bob Church *(Chapter IV)*
Burlington Technical Center, Automotive Science and Technology
Instructor, Vermont

Tina Cox *(Chapter X)*
Kern High School District, Regional Occupational Center, Early
Childhood Education Instructor, California

Monique Currie *(Chapter I)*
Wisconsin Technical College System, Policy Advisor, Wisconsin

Lisa Greenawalt, Ed.D. *(Chapter VIII)*
Lehigh Career and Technical Institute, Director of Curriculum and
Instruction, Pennsylvania

Michelle MacIntosh *(Chapter II)*
California Department of Education, Education Administrator,
California

Shawn McDermott *(Chapter I)*
Lake Region Vocational Center, Law Enforcement Instructor, Maine

Kathleen McNally, Ph.D. *(Chapter V)*
Southern Regional Education Board (SREB), School Improvement
Specialist, Georgia

Michelle Means-Walker, Ed.D. *(Chapter V)*
Educational Consultant, Ohio

Kristen Pearson, M.Ed. *(Chapter VII)*
Western Maricopa Education Center, Professional Development Specialist, Arizona

Kyle Peck, Ph.D. *(Chapter X)*
Penn State University, Center for Online Learning and Innovation
Director, Pennsylvania

Brian Peffley, CEPC, CCE, AAC *(Chapter IV)*
Lebanon County Career and Technology Center, Pastry Arts Instructor,
Pennsylvania

Doug Sands *(Chapter II)*
United Technical Center, Machine Tool Technology Instructor, West
Virginia

Eric Showalter *(Chapter IV)*
Washburn University, Technical Instructor, Kansas

Bill Sorenson *(Chapter III)*
Stanly County Schools, Technology Instructor, North Carolina

Natasha Rae Telger *(Chapter VII)*
Southern Illinois University Carbondale Center for Workforce
Development, Integration and Training Coordinator, Illinois

Delmas Watkins, Ed.D. *(Chapter IX)*
DeKalb County School District, CTAE Director, Student Advancement,
Georgia

Russell Weikle, M.A. *(Chapter VI)*
Educational Consultant, California

Contributing Organizations

The authors would like to both recognize and thank ACTE and NOCTI for their contributions and assistance with this book. Unlike the individuals recognized in the previous section, these entities provided the authors with the opportunity to expand their individual knowledge and skills and have indirectly influenced much of the content of this book through conversations and interviews with their members and clients. In addition, these organizations have contributed resources, both human and financial, to make this book a reality.

ACTE (The Association for Career and Technical Education)
The Association for Career and Technical Education is the largest national education association in the United States and is dedicated to the advancement of education that prepares youth and adults for careers. ACTE was founded in 1926, and it has remained committed to enhancing the job performance and satisfaction of its members; to increasing public awareness and appreciation for CTE; and to assuring growth in local, state, and federal funding for these programs by communicating and working with legislators and government leaders.

NOCTI (Formerly the National Occupational Competency Testing Institute)
NOCTI is an assessment organization that was founded in the mid-1960s as a not-for-profit entity serving the CTE field through a consortium made up of CTE directors (or their designees) from each state and U.S. territory. NOCTI shares the objective of other CTE associations, including Advance CTE, who elect the NOCTI board of directors, and ACTE, whose membership this book is targeted to assist. All three organizations have expertise in, and a strong commitment to, improving America's workforce.

Special Thanks

Amie L. Bloomfield, B.S., NOCTI, Executive Vice President
for additional editing and creative development

Carol L. Hodes, Ph.D., NOCTI, Senior Consultant
for searching the literature for resources that are useful to CTE teachers

Alisha D. Hyslop, ACTE, Director of Public Policy
for her insightful contributions to the chapters on federal legislation

Jaclyn D. Kamp, NOCTI, Lead Graphic Designer
for her creative illustrations and suggestions

Kathleen P. McNally, Ph.D., SREB, School Improvement Specialist
for her insight in several of the chapters regarding instructional strategies

Sandra G. Pritz, Ph.D., NOCTI, Senior Consultant
for many hours spent checking consistency, tone, style, and grammar

Complete Resource List

Advance CTE. (2016). State Leaders Connecting Learning to Work. https://www.careertech.org/.

ACTE. (2016, July). *Leveraging Intermediaries to Expand Work Based Learning.* Available at https://careertech.org/sites/default/files/files/resources/WBL_casestudy_Intermediaries_FINAL.pdf.

ACTE. (2008, March). Career and technical education's role in workforce readiness credentials. *ACTE Issue Brief.* Available at www.acteonline.org.

American Culinary Federation. (2016). Certify. Available at www.acfchefs.org/ACF/Certify.

American Management Association. (2010). *AMA 2010 Critical Skills Survey.* Available at http://www.amanet.org/.

Andrade, G., Huff, K. & Brooke, G. (2012). *Assessment in the Context of Student-centered Learning: The Students at the Center Series.* Boston, MA: Jobs for the Future. Available at http://www.jff.org/sites/default/files/publications/materials/Assessing%20LearningPDF.pdf.

Assessment.com. (2016). *Career Test for High School Students. Career Test for College Students (MAPP Career Test).* Available at http://www.assessment.com/Students-Graduates.asp.

Association for Career and Technical Education (ACTE). (2006). *Perkins Act of 2006: The Official Guide.* Alexandria, VA: Author.

Association for Career and Technical Education (ACTE). (2016). *Connecting Education and Careers.* Available at www.acteonline.org/join.

Baden-Powell, R. (1941). AZ Quotes. Available at http://www.azquotes.com/author/759-Robert_Baden_Powell.

Blackboard Schoolwires. (2002-2016). *Integrated Academics.* Blackboard, Inc. Available at www.vbisd.org/Page/547.

Bock, S. H. (2010, January). Teacher recognition. *Techniques. (85)*1, Pp 30-33.

Brookings Institution. (2013). The Hidden STEM Economy. Retrieved from http://www.brookings.edu/research/interactives/2013/the-hidden-stem-economy.

Buck Institute for Education (BIE). (2016). Why Project Based Learning (PBL)? Available at http://www.bie.org.

California Department of Education. (n.d.). Standards for Career Ready Practice. Available at http://www.cde.ca.gov/ci/ct/sf/documents/ctescrpflyer.pdf.

Carl D. Perkins Career and Technical Education Act of 2006 (Perkins IV). (Public Law 109-270).

Carl D. Perkins Career and Technical Education Act of 1998 (Perkins III). (Public Law 105-332).

Carl D. Perkins Career and Technical Education Act of 1990 (Perkins II). (Public Law 101-392).

Carl D. Perkins Vocational Education Act of 1984. (Public Law 98-524).

Carnevale, A. (2016, May 31). Credentials and Competencies: Demonstrating The Economic Value of Post-secondary Education. Parchment Summit on Innovating Academic Credentials. Available at https://cew.georgetown.edu/publications/journals-articles/.

Cole, B. (2014). Chapter V: Sometimes you have to build fences. In Cole, B., Foster, J., Foster, P. & McNally, K., *Your First Year in CTE: Ten Things to Know,* pp. 32-37. Alexandria, VA: ACTE.

Cole, B., Foster, J.C., Foster, P. & McNally, K. (2014). *Your First Year in CTE: 10 things to know.* Alexandria, VA: ACTE.

Colorado Technology Student Association. (2016). *The benefits of implementing a career and technical student organization.* Available at www.cotsa.cccs.edu.

Competency-Based Education Network. (2016). *What is Competency-Based Education?* Available at http://www.cbenetwork.org/.

Council on Occupational Education (COE). (2016). *The Self-Study Manual,2016 Edition.* Atlanta, GA: Author. Available at http://www.council.org/manuals/.

Danielson, C. (2008). *The handbook for enhancing professional practice: using the framework for teaching in your school.* ASCD: Alexandria, VA.

Danielson, C. (1999). Mentoring beginning teachers: The case for mentoring. *Teaching and Change,* 6(3), pp. 251-257.

DiMaria, F. (2016, April 16). Allowing technology to amplify quality teaching. *THE Journal.* Available at https://thejournal.com/articles/2016/04/20/allowing-technology-to-amplify-quality-teaching.aspx.

Duncan, A. (2011, February 2). *The new CTE: Secretary Duncan's prepared remarks at the release of the "Pathways to Prosperity" report.* Available at http://www.ed.gov/news/speeches/new-cte-secretary-duncans-remarks-career-and-technical-education.

EdWeek Webinar Archive. (2016, March 8). Go Digital with Formative Assessment & Critical Thinking. Available at https://vts.inxpo.com/scripts/Server.nxp?LASCmd=AI:4;F:QS!10100&ShowKey=30157&partnerref=TOC&Referrer=http%3A%2F%2Fwww.edweek.org%2Few%2Fmarketplace%2Fwebinars%2Fwebinars.html.

Edutopia. (2016). Resources. Available at http://www.edutopia.org/.

Elementary and Secondary Education Act (Every Student Succeeds Act). (2015). S. 1177–114th Congress: PL 114-95. Available at https://www.gpo.gov/fdsys/pkg/BILLS-114s1177enr/pdf/BILLS-114s1177enr.pdf.

Elgart, M.A. (2016, September). Creating state accountability systems that help schools improve. *Phi Delta Kappan,* 98(1) 26-30.

Employment and Training Administration. (2016, February 25). Competency Models. Available at https://www.doleta.gov/usworkforce/uswf_nav.cfm#Competency.

Ennis, M., & Showerman, R. (2011). *Online resources to support academic & CTE integration.* Presented at Michigan Career Conference. Available at www.michigancareerconference.org.

Field, S, (2016, June 3). *Scaffolding Content and Process in PBL.* Buck Institute for Education. Available at http://www.bie.org/blog/scaffolding_content_and_process_in_pbl.

Foster, J.C., Foster, P., Hornberger, C. & McNally, K. (2015). *Your First Year in CTE: 10 More Things to Know.* Alexandria, VA: ACTE.

Foster, J., Hodes, C.L., & Pritz, S.G. (2014). *Putting your data to work: Improving instruction in CTE.* Alexandria, VA: ACTE.

Green, A. (2013, July 22). What does it mean to be professional at work? *U.S. News and World Report*, On Careers Blog. Available at http://money.usnews.com/money/blogs/outside-voices-careers/2013/07/22/what-does-it-mean-to-be-professional-at-work.

Greenberg, A., & Nilssen, A. (2015, April). The role of education in building soft skills. *Wainhouse Research, LLC.* Available at cp.wainhouse.com/content/role-education-building-soft-skills.

Heiser, E.A. (2016, September). CBE in CTE: The Perfect Fit. *Techniques. 91*(6), 14-18. Available at www.acteonline.org.

Hodge, K., & Lear, J. (2011). Employment skills for 21st century workplace: the gap between faculty and student perceptions. *Journal of Career and Technical Education. 26*(2), Available at ejournals.lib.vt.edu.

Hoffman, R. (2013, September 16). Disrupting the diploma. *LinkedIn Pulse.* Available at https://www.linkedin.com/pulse/20130916065028-1213-disrupting-the-diploma.

Holzer, H. (2015, April). *Job Market Polarization and U.S. Worker Skills: A Tale of Two Middles.* Washington, DC: The Brookings Institution. Available at https://www.brookings.edu/research/job-market-polarization-and-u-s-worker-skills-a-tale-of-two-middles/.

Huguet, M. C. (2016, April). A Blended Approach. *Techniques. 91*(4), 28-32. Available at www.acteonline.org.

Industrial Maintenance and Plant Operation. (2015, June). Jobs Report 2015. *IMPO.* Available at www.impomag.com.

International Society for Technology in Education (ISTE). (2009). *Digital age leadership, Standards for Teachers.* Available at http://www.iste.org/standards/standards/standards-for-teachers.

Jackson, D. (2016). Standards for professional learning. *Learning Forward.* Available at https://learningforward.org/standards/leadership.

Jobs for the Future & the Council of Chief State School Officers. (2015, August). *Educator Competencies for Personalized, Learner-Centered Teaching.* Boston, MA: Jobs for the Future. Available at http://files.eric.ed.gov/fulltext/ED560785.pdf.

Kansas State Department of Education. (2013, September). Resource List of Industry-Recognized Assessments/Certifications/Credentials. Topeka, KS: Author. Available at http://www.ksde.org/Portals/0/CSAS/CSAS%20Home/CTE%20Home/Career_Cluster_Pathway/Industry%20Cert%20Resource%20List%209-11-13.pdf?ver=2013-09-11-104018-430.

Klein-Collins, R. (2010). Fueling the Race to Post-secondary Success: A 48-Institution Study of Prior Learning Assessment and Adult Student Outcomes. Chicago, IL: Council for Adult and Experiential Learning. Available at http://cdn2.hubspot.net/hubfs/617695/premium_content_resources/pla/PDF/PLA_Fueling-the-Race.pdf.

Krovetz, M. (2016, March). Expecting All Students and Educators to Use the Hearts and Minds Well. *Educational Leadership and Administration: Teaching and Program Development,* v27, 231-242. ERIC Number: EJ1094429.

Kuchinke, K. (1999). Workforce education faculty as leaders: do graduate-level university instructors exhibit transformational leadership behaviors? *Journal of Vocational Education Research, 24*(4) 209-225.

Lakein, A. (1989). *How to Get Control of Your Time and Your Life.* Signet Books. New York: New York.

Lakin, M., Nellum, D., Seymour, C. & Crandall, J. (2015). Credit for Prior Learning: Charting Institutional Practice for Sustainability. Washington, DC: American Council on Education. Available at https://www.acenet.edu/news-room/Documents/Credit-for-Prior-Learning-Charting-Institutional-Practice-for-Sustainability.pdf.

Leithwood, K., Louis, K. S., Anderson, S., & Wahlstrom, K. (2004). How Leadership Influences Student Learning. Available at http://www.wallacefoundation.org/ knowledge-center/school-leadership/keyresearch/Documents/How-Leadership-Influences-Student-Learning.pdf.

Manufacturing Skills Standards Council. (2016). *Manufacturing Skill Standards Certification (MSSC) For Employers.* Kenosha, WI: Author. Available at https://www.gtc.edu/business-workforce-solutions/certifications/mssc.

McKay, D. (2015, November 24). Soft skills: what they are and why you need them. *About. com.* Available at www.careerplanning.about.com.

Middle States Association of Colleges and Schools. (2012). Standards for Career and Technical Institutions. Philadelphia, PA: Author. Available at http://www.msa-cess.org/Customized/uploads/Accreditation/Standards%20for%20Accreditation-CT%20Institutions%202012.pdf.

MindTools. (1996-2016). Why soft skills matter: making sure your hard skills shine. Available at https://www.mindtools.com/pages/article/newCDV_34.htm.

Mordan, B.R. (2012, December). *Retention and Professional Mentoring of Beginning Career and Technical Education Teachers.* Pennsylvania State University. Unpublished dissertation. Available at https://etda.libraries.psu.edu/files/final_submissions/7966.

Moye, J. (2011, March). Real integration—where the rubber meets the road. *Techniques, 86*(3), 48-51. Available at www.acteonline.org.

National Association of Colleges and Employers (NACE). (2016). *Career Readiness Defined: NACE defines career readiness, identifies key competencies.* Available at http://www.naceweb.org/knowledge/career-readiness-competencies.aspx.

National Association of Home Builders. (2016). *Course Overviews.* Available at http://www.nahb.org/en/learn/course-overviews.aspx.

National Association of State Boards of Education. (1998, October). *The numbers game: Ensuring Quantity and Quality in The Teaching Workforce.* The Report of The NASBE Study Group on Teacher Development, Supply, and Demand. Alexandria, VA: Author. Available at http://nasbe.org/wp-content/uploads/SG_Numbers_Game_1_Teacher_Development_1998.pdf

National Board for Professional Teaching Standards. (2014). *NBPTS Career and Technical Education Standards, second edition.* Arlington, VA: Author. Available at http://boardcertifiedteachers.org/sites/default/files/EAYA-CTE.pdf.

National Career Development Association. (2016). *Internet Sites for Career Planning.* Available at www.ncda.org/aws/NCDA/pt/sp/resources.

National College Credit Recommendation Service (NCCRS). (2016). Cooperating Colleges and Universities. Available at http://www.nationalccrs.org/organizations/nocti-and-nocti-business.

National Research Center for Career and Technical Education (NRCCTE). (n.d.). Career Pathways and Programs of Study, The National Research Center for Career and Technical Education at the Southern Regional Education Board. Available at http://www.nrccte.org/core-issues/programs-study.

Neves, A. (2016). 5 Skills you need to work on to get ahead—No matter what industry you're in. *Daily Muse.* Available at https://www.themuse.com/advice/5-skills-you-need-to-work-on-to-get-aheadno-matter-what-industry-youre-in.

Nunn, R. (2016, June 21). *Occupational Licensing and the American Worker.* Washington, DC: The Brookings Institution. Available at https://www.brookings.edu/research/occupational-licensing-and-the-american-worker/.

Office of Career Technical and Adult Education (OCTAE). (2016). Employability Skills Framework. U.S. Department of Education: Washington, DC. Available at http://cte.ed.gov/employabilityskills/.

Office of Career Technical and Adult Education (OCTAE). (2016). Lesson Planning Checklist. Available at http://cte.ed.gov/employabilityskills/index.php/developingskills/create_checklist.

O*Net. (2016). O*Net Interest Profiler. Washington, DC: U.S. Department of Labor. Available at http://www.mynextmove.org/explore/ip.

PA Department of Education. (2013). SOAR Flyer. Available at http://www.education.pa.gov/Documents/K-12/Career%20and%20Technical%20Education/Programs%20of%20Study/SOAR%20Flyer.pdf.

PA Department of Education. (2014). *Cooperative Education Guidelines for Administration: How to Comply with Federal and State Laws and Regulations.* Harrisburg, PA: Author. Available at http://www.education.pa.gov/Documents/K-12/Career%20and%20Technical%20Education/Teacher%20Resources/Cooperative%20Education/How%20to%20Comply%20with%20Federal%20and%20State%20Laws%20and%20Regulations.pdf.

Partnership for 21ˢᵗ Century Skills (P21). (2016). Framework for 21st Century Learning. Available at http://www.p21.org/our-work/p21-framework.

Pathways to Prosperity State Network. (2014, June). *State Progress Report, 2012-2014.* Jobs for the Future: Boston, MA. ED561260.

Patrick, S. & Sturgis, C. (2015, March). Maximizing competency sducation and blended learning. *Competency Works Issue Brief.* Vienna, VA: International Association for K-12 Online Learning. Available through http://eric.ed.gov/ number ED557755.

Pawlowski, B. (2016, March). Finding and Engaging Business Partners, *Techniques, 91*(3), pp. 14-17. Available at www.acteonline.org.

Peck, K. L. (2013, Fall). Measuring success: Reinventing the report card. *AdvancED.* Available at http://www.advanc-ed.org/source/reinventing-report-card.

Pennsylvania Association of Career and Technical Administrators (PACTA). (2016). Resources. Available at http://www.pacareertech.org/resources/categories.

Pennsylvania Department of Education. (2016). Pennsylvania Academic Standards Crosswalk, Grade 11. Available at http://www.education.pa.gov/K-12/PACareerStandards/Curriculum/Pages/Crosswalks.aspx#tab-1.

Pennsylvania Department of Education. (2014a). *Comprehensive Planning Career and Technical Center Planning Offline Guidance Tool.* Harrisburg, PA: Author. Available at http://compplanning.wiki.caiu.org/home.

Pennsylvania Department of Education. (2014b). Educator Effectiveness Administrative Manual. Harrisburg, PA: Author. Available at http://www.education.pa.gov/Documents/Teachers-Administrators/Educator%20Effectiveness/Educator%20Effectiveness%20Administrative%20Manual.pdf.

Perkins Collaborative Resource Network. (2016a). Accountability: Annual reporting. Available at http://cte.ed.gov/accountability/annual-reporting.

Perkins Collaborative Resource Network. (2016b). Legislation: Workforce Innovation and Opportunity Act (WIOA). Washington, DC: U.S. Department of Education. Available at http://cte.ed.gov/legislation/about-wioa.

Perkins Collaborative Resource Network. (2016c). Legislation: Every Student Succeeds Act (ESSA). Washington, DC: U.S. Department of Education. Available at http://cte.ed.gov/legislation/about-essa.

Philpot, D. (2010, October 27). Soft skills: more important than you might think! *Texas Education Agency, Career and Technical Education Blog.* Available at http://cte-unt.blogspot.com/2010/10/soft-skills-more-important-than-you.html.

Post, P. (2014, August 17). Traits that convey character also define a professional. *Boston Globe, Business Section.* Available at https://www.bostonglobe.com/business/2014/08/16/just-what-does-mean-professional/MTlZfzUhw4cDphH6E99LIO/story.html.

Rickabaugh, J. (2015). Including the learner in personalized learning. *Connect: Making Learning Personal Issue Brief.* Center on Innovations in Learning, Philadelphia, PA: Temple University. Available through http://eric.ed.gov/ ED558048.

Robinson, G. (2016, July 27). Presentations and portfolios take the place of tests for some students. *Hechinger Report.* http://hechingerreport.org/presentations-and-portfolios-take-the-place-of-tests-for-some-students/.

Rodman, M. (2012). *A Study of Learning-centered Leadership Skills of Principals in Career and Technical Education Schools.* Pennsylvania State University. Unpublished dissertation available at https://etda.libraries.psu.edu/files/final_submissions/7033.

Rosenberg, H. (2013). Embracing the use of data for continuous program improvement. *Family Involvement Network of Educators (FINE) Newsletter, 5*(3). Retrieved September 6, 2016, from http://www.hfrp.org/family-involvement/fine-family-involvement-network-of-educators/fine-newsletter-archive/september-fine-newsletter-creating-a-culture-of-continuous-improvement.

Salemi, V. (2016, January 12). 4 Traits that a hiring manages wants in a new employee. *U.S. News and World Report,* On Careers Blog. Available at http://money.usnews.com/money/blogs/outside-voices-careers/articles/2016-01-12/4-traits-that-hiring-managers-want-in-a-new-employee.

Schwartz, R. B. (2014, Fall). The pursuit of pathways: Combining rigorous academics with career training. *American Educator,* pp 24-29, 41.

Shumer, R., & Digby, C. (2012, January). The future of CTE: Programs of study. *Techniques: Connecting Education and Careers, 87*(1) 36-39. EJ976604.

Skills You Need Newsletter. (2011-2016). What Are Soft Skills? Available http://www.skillsyouneed.com/general/soft-skills.html.

Smith-Hughes Act. (2016). In *Encyclopædia Britannica.* Retrieved from https://www.britannica.com/topic/Smith-Hughes-Act.

Stahl, R.J. (1994, March). The Essential Elements of Cooperative Learning in the Classroom. *ERIC Digest.* ED370881. Available at http://www.ericdigests.org/1995-1/elements.htm.

Stipanovic, N., Shumer, R., & Stringfield, S. (2012). Lessons learned from highly implemented programs of study, *Techniques: Connecting Education and Careers, 87*(1) 21-23. EJ976600.

Sussman, A. L. (2016, September 1). As skill requirements increase, more manufacturing jobs go unfilled. *The Wall Street Journal.* Available at http://www.wsj.com/.

The College Foundation of West Virginia. (2016). *Career Planning.* Charleston, WV: Author. Available at https://secure.cfwv.com/Career_Planning/_default.aspx.

Threeton, M.D. (2007, Spring). The Carl D. Perkins Career and Technical Education (CTE) Act of 2006 and the roles and responsibilities of CTE teachers and faculty members. *Journal of Industrial Teacher Education, 44*(1). Available at http://scholar.lib.vt.edu/ejournals/JITE/v44n1/threeton.html.

Tough, P. (2016, June). How kids learn resilience, *The Atlantic*. Available at
http://www.theatlantic.com/magazine/toc/2016/06/.

U.S. Army. (2016). U.S. Army Careers and Jobs. Washington, DC: Author. Available at
http://www.goarmy.com/careers-and-jobs.html.

U.S. Department of Education. (2016). *Career and Technical Student Organizations*. Office of
Career, Technical and Adult Education. Last modified: 01/27/2016. Available at
http://www2.ed.gov/about/offices/list/ovae/pi/cte/vso.html.

U.S. Department of Education, Office of the Under Secretary, Policy and Program Studies
Service. (2004). *National Assessment of Vocational Education: Final Report to Congress,* Washington, D.C.: Author.

U.S. Department of Education. (2016). The Federal Role in Education. Washington, DC:
Author. Available at http://www2.ed.gov/about/overview/fed/role.html.

Viviano, T. (2012, Winter). What 21st century leadership in career and technical education
should look like. *Journal of Career and Technical Education, 27*(2) 51-56. EJ995894

Walker, D. (2012, Nov.–Dec.). Building robust community partnerships. *Techniques, 87*(8)
pp 36-38. Available at www.acteonline.org.

Watson, J., Murin, A., Vashaw, L., Gemin, B., & Rapp, C. (2013). *Keeping Pace with K-12
Online & Blended Learning: An Annual Review of Policy and Practice, 2013*. Grand Rapids, MI:
Evergreen Education Group. Available at http://files.eric.ed.gov/fulltext/ED565714.pdf

Wells, A. (2014). Why The Manufacturing Skills Gap Is Serious. Manufacturing Net. Available at http://www.manufacturing.net/blog/2014/06/why-manufacturing-skills-gap-serious

West Virginia Office of Career Technical Education. (2016). Simulated Workplace. Charleston, WV: WV Department of Education (WVDE). Available at http://wvde.state.wv.us/
simulated-workplace/.

West Virginia Department of Education. (2016). Teacher Resources. Charleston, WV: Author.
Available at http://wvde.state.wv.us/counselors/links/curriculum/delivery-resources.html.

West Virginia Department of Education. (2016). *Learning, Individualized Needs, Knowledge
and Skills* (The LINKS program). Charleston, WV: Author. Available at http://wvde.state.
wv.us/counselors/links/about.html.

Wonacott, M. (2001). Leadership Development in Career and Technical Education. *ERIC
Digest No. 225*. ED452366 2001-00-00. Available at http://eric.ed.gov/.

Workforce Innovation and Opportunity Act (WIOA). (2014). Public Law 113-128 (29
U.S.C. Sec. 3101, et. seq.). Retrieved from https://www.doleta.gov/wioa/Docs/WIOA_FAQs_
Round2.pdf.

Young, J., Cline, F., King, T., Jackson, A. & Timberlake, A. (2011, August). *High Schools
That Work: Program Description, Literature Review, and Research Findings*. Princeton, NJ: Educational Testing Service.

Zetlin, M. (2014, December). 9 Secrets to effective networking, even if you're a nerd. *Inc.*
Available at http://www.inc.com/minda-zetlin/9-secrets-to-effective-networking-even-if-you-
re-a-nerd.html.